Three Minutes a Day

Volume 29

Feed the Hungry

*Share what you have with those who need it,
down the street and around the world.*

Donated by

Dr. Linda Barrasse

Att. Joe Cosgrove

Other Christopher Books in Print

Three Minutes a Day
V. 28 in the series

Three Minutes a Day
V. 27 in the series

The Best of Three Minutes a Day (Volumes 6-10)
V. 26 in the series

Enjoy the Lord
A Path to Contemplation

God Delights in You
An Introduction to Gospel Spirituality

God Is Unchanging Love

World Religions
Beliefs Behind Today's Headlines

You Are the Light of the World

Three Minutes a Day

29th volume in a series containing inspirational stories and reflections for each day of the year.

Father John Catoir

Director, The Christophers

Stephanie Raha

Editor-in-Chief

Margaret O'Connell
Mary Riddle

Associate Editors

Alison Moran

Media Associate

THE CHRISTOPHERS, 12 East 48th Street, New York, NY 10017

ISBN # 0 - 939055 - 02 - 3

The law of the Lord is perfect,
reviving the soul;
the testimony of the Lord is sure,
making wise the simple;
the precepts of the Lord are right,
rejoicing the heart.
. . . More to be desired are they than gold
. . . sweeter also than honey.

Psalm 19:7-8,10

Introduction

It is a great delight for me to bring you this 29th volume in The Christophers' THREE MINUTES A DAY series.

The purpose of each edition remains the same: to share with you the idealism and hope that is the essence of the Christopher message. You will find in these pages 365 reminders that God loves you completely and eternally, and that He has a particular mission for you.

And so we offer you these readings to nourish your soul as you try to respond generously to God's calling. Some pages might make you smile, others will inform you, but all will encourage you to reflect on your role in the larger scheme of things. You are essential to God's plan of salvation.

Our loving Lord counts on us to value, respect and care for one another and all creation. And The Christophers will be at your side to offer you an encouraging word, one that will lead you ever closer to the Word of God Who is the source of our strength and our life.

Love and prayers,

Father John Catoir

The work of His hands

Here's some good advice from a second century bishop, Irenaeus of Lyon, about our relationship with God.

... you are the work of God,
   await the hand of the Artist
who does all things in due season.
Offer Him your heart, soft and
   tractable and keep the form in
which the Artist has fashioned you.
Let the clay (of your being) be moist,
   lest you grow hard
   And lose the imprint
   of His fingers.

Centuries before, the prophet Jeremiah had written that we are like clay in the potter's hand — God's hand. We need only be patient and eager to be shaped by our Maker.

Can I not do with you as this potter has done? says the Lord. Behold, like the clay in the potter's hand, so are you in My hand. (Jeremiah 18:6)

Master Potter, form me, fashion me, into a fit vessel for Your Spirit.

Your truth, my truth, and real truth

A Beverly Hills psychiatrist recently commented that he wished modern technology could produce a tape recorder that would be activated automatically by behavior that leads to arguments.

A recording of what actually takes place during conflicts would obviously be valuable to psychiatrists. They now have to analyze a conflict from two different — and often contradictory — accounts of what happened.

When it comes to arguments, memory's not very reliable. It exaggerates the anger and spite in the other person's remarks and softens the harshness of our own. Hearing what we really said might be a shock.

It's all too easy to let anger take control and lead to hurtful words — words that only increase conflict. Kindness and respect for the feelings of the other person are essential in settling differences of any kind.

Your anger does not produce God's righteousness. (James 1:20)

While anger is a normal emotion, Jesus, enable me to channel it in healthy ways.

A great singer

Opera singer Luigi Lablache was considered the greatest bass of the mid-nineteenth century. But opera then offered few leading roles for a bass, so between leads, he sang minor parts.

A colleague once remarked that Lablache was wasted in the small part he was singing at the time. Lablache replied, "My friend, to a great singer there are no small parts. And to a small singer there are no great ones."

Sometimes we may feel that our role in life is only a small one. But *every* role is important when it's done well — in opera and in life.

> **To each is given the manifestation of the Spirit for the common good.**
> **(1 Corinthians 12:7)**

> *Giver of every good gift, inspire us to use our gifts for the common good.*

God's special protection

God cares for all His creatures, including African four-striped grass mice. These striped beauties brave the fiery sun of Africa's Kalahari Desert to find choice seeds and leaves. And they do not suffer sunstroke.

It seems that beneath their gold and black fur their skin is black. This pigment shields these mice from the sun's harmful ultraviolet radiation.

They also wear black skull caps — a layer of black tissue between brains and skin — for extra protection.

Consider how perfectly these wee mice have been created for their harsh environment.

God does indeed care for us, guarding us as the apples of His eye.

And each moment of each day is proof of that.

The Lord's own portion was His people, Jacob His allotted share. . . . He shielded him, cared for him, guarded him as the apple of His eye. (Deuteronomy 32:9,10)

Guard me, Heavenly Parent, as the apple of Your eye.

Really respecting others

We show our respect for each person we meet through our sensitivity to their needs and feelings. Curiosity and ignorance can drive us to say or do foolish, even harmful, things. Tactless comments, questions or jokes about another's looks, background, beliefs or behavior can hurt. And saying that we didn't mean it just isn't enough.

Judith Martin, the etiquette expert known as Miss Manners, offers this thought: "Putting yourself in another person's place means imagining that person's point of view, not just thinking of what you, with your ideas, would do in the other person's situation."

That's an interesting perspective. It's worth bearing in mind that a thoughtful attitude transforms good intentions into genuine kindness.

And nothing in the world substitutes for the warmth of genuine kindness.

Clothe yourselves with compassion, kindness, humility, meekness, and patience. Bear with one another and . . . forgive each other. (Colossians 3:12-13)

You've always been kind to me, Jesus. How may I be kind to others today?

Seeing all life's colors

Some people literally see the world in a rosier light than others.

Apples and rubies and fire engines look redder to them. And their eyes can distinguish slight variations in the shades of red between, say, two red shirts that look identical to other people.

Recent studies show that a difference in just one amino acid makes this difference in color vision. It affects the way certain specialized cells of the eye absorb red light.

How we see *color* is determined by heredity. It's beyond our control.

But how we see *life* is up to us. We can choose to live joyfully no matter what our circumstances — by trusting in God's love.

> **Thus says the Lord . . . 'Fear not, for I have redeemed you; I have called you by name, you are Mine . . . you are precious in My eyes, and honored, and I love you.'**
> **(Isaiah 43:1,4)**

Creator and Redeemer, You do love me and protect me. May I appreciate Your love!

Just for today

I'd like to share some "just for today" suggestions for you to take to work with you. Just for today . . .

- be as friendly as possible with co-workers
- try to see the good in every situation
- find something to praise in every person
- be happy you're alive, well and employed
- do not compare yourself with anyone else
- leave work looking forward to the evening, thankful for what you've accomplished
- have no expectations about how you should be treated
- try to help out in every situation

Just for today . . . and tomorrow . . . and the next day. Soon your world would be a better place for your being in it. And after all isn't that the one thing we can all accomplish — just for today?

Jesus of Nazareth . . . went about doing good. (Acts 10:38)

Inspired by Your example, Jesus, may we also do good.

Two donkeys reach one solution

A cartoon strip drawn for the Quaker Peace and Service group in England makes an important point with a few simple drawings. And it's understandable to people regardless of what language they speak.

The cartoon shows two donkeys standing chained together between two piles of hay. Each donkey pulls with all its might, trying to reach the hay on its side. But since they are pulling in opposite directions, neither gets anywhere.

Finally, they give up and sit looking at each other. Then they have an idea. Together they walk to one pile of hay and eat it. Then they walk together to the other pile.

Between individuals or between nations, cooperation is the key to solving problems.

Resolve instead never to put a stumbling block or hindrance in the way of another . . . pursue what makes for peace and for mutual upbuilding. (Romans 14:13,19)

Help us learn cooperation, Prince of Peace.

Leaping time

Got a second? Well, every once in a while you lose one, probably without knowing it.

Telling time over the centuries has depended on our astronomical observations. The changes in the positions of the sun and stars has, in fact, indicated the rotation of the earth on its axis.

But, the earth is not constant. It picks up speed or slows down in unpredictable ways. We don't even know why, though the gravitational attraction of the sun and moon as well as atmospheric conditions play a part.

So atomic clocks are more accurate because they use fixed reference points called quasars. And every once in a while, the difference between atomic and solar time is made up with a "leap second."

However time is measured, its value is always up to you. Use it well today and tomorrow.

So teach us to count our days that we may gain a wise heart. (Psalm 90:12)

Give us that wisdom which sits by Your throne, God.

A little list

Here's a list of "little mores" to help make your life a "little more" God-centered:

● a little more PATIENCE with this difficult person . . .

● a little more FIRMNESS with repellent work . . .

● a little more COMMON SENSE to accept people as they are . . .

● a little more STRENGTH to endure what's disturbing . . .

● a little more CHEERFULNESS when hurt and upset . . .

● a little more UNSELFISHNESS when understanding others . . .

● a little more PRUDENCE not to become a busy-body . . .

and . . .

● a little more PRAYER to talk over things with God.

Not only will your life be a "little more" God-centered, it'll be a "little more" people-centered.

I prayed, and understanding was given me; I called on God, and the spirit of wisdom came to me. (Wisdom of Solomon 7:7)

Come, Spirit of God Most High, come.

Build up, don't belittle

Writer Robert Fulghum added a wise twist to an old saying. "Sticks and stones may break our bones," he suggests, "but words will break our hearts."

It's true. What we say about others and to them can make a big difference for better or worse. Rude or degrading insults based on a person's background, beliefs, looks or behavior have no place in mature conversation. Because people are never as simple as the language we use to describe them, stereotypes do an injustice to others — and to our better selves.

Verbal attacks belittle and debilitate by treading on another's self-worth.

But just as ridicule, labels and put-downs can hurt, other words can help. Praise and encouragement, comfort and compliments can make any one's day.

> **Let no evil talk come out of your mouths, but only what is useful for building up. (Ephesians 4:29)**

> *Spirit of Wisdom, how may I build up those with whom I talk today?*

Learning to inherit society

The problem with American education, says Professor Kevin Walsh of the University of Alabama, is not that Johnny isn't being taught to read and write and do math. The problem is that Johnny isn't being taught values and self-discipline.

"The purpose of education," says Walsh, "is to prepare the next generation to inherit society." He considers values and self-discipline basic to character, self-esteem, and success in jobs.

As a member of the county board of education, he's putting his ideas into practice in public schools in the towns of Trussville and Hewitt. The result has been a dramatic increase in students' motivation to learn.

Teaching young people sound values and a positive attitude is a priceless gift to them.

> **Discipline your (child) while there is hope; do not set your heart on his destruction. (Proverbs 19:18)**

> *Wisdom of the Father, enlighten and encourage teachers and members of boards of education to make sound educational decisions.*

For the love of Christ

An elderly blind man was selling pencils in midtown Manhattan when a taxi jumped the curb and struck him and his guide dog, injuring both. The man was taken to a hospital and his Labrador to an animal hospital.

The Labrador received hundreds of cards, many with money enclosed for his care, and as many as 400 people a day called to ask about him. His master got only a handful of get-well cards and had very few calls or visitors.

While dogs can be lovable and deserve our care, a person is infinitely more precious. We may need to look beyond the effects of age and circumstances and handicaps to see the beauty of Christ in another, but it is there. And in helping another person, we help Christ.

You have made (mortals) a little lower than God. (Psalm 8:5)

Blessed may You be, God my Creator, for having knit me in Your image and likeness!

"Show something different"

"A Woman's Tale" is a movie with an unusual premise. The film is about a dying woman, starring a dying woman.

The movie was directed by Paul Cox and stars Sheila Florance, who was dying of cancer when the film was made. The story is about a frail but spirited old woman who shares her undying love with friends and strangers alike. Sheila Florance lived long enough to receive the Australian Oscar for best actress. She died a week after accepting the award.

Paul Cox felt that "A Woman's Tale" was a movie that had to be made. "I realize that I live in a society where the words 'gentleness' and 'tenderness' have all but disappeared," he said. Movies tend to "celebrate people who show how tough they are and how big their biceps are, and so it's my duty to show something different."

It's the duty of each of us "to show something different." Try to spread a little kindness in your community.

Although You are sovereign in strength, You judge with mildness, and with great forbearance. (Wisdom of Solomon 12:18)

That we might imitate your mildness and "great forbearance," Merciful and Compassionate Lord.

The dream continues

Speaking of Rev. Dr. Martin Luther King, Jr., recently deceased Archbishop James P. Lyke said, "He had a profound effect on my life . . . his ideals of the unity of the human family . . . He would enter neighborhoods and challenge people to be true to themselves.

"If we had talked to white Catholics about what it really means to be a Catholic — staying in neighborhoods, welcoming people of other cultures, racial, ethnic and religious backgrounds — then we wouldn't have these problems in . . . Detroit, Chicago, Newark, New York, Cleveland, Atlanta . . . What African-American, Hispanic and Asian people are experiencing now, in too many instances, is not authentic faith. They experience exclusion."

Dr. King said "I have a dream." Whatever our religion or heritage, is Dr. King's dream of the unity within the human family our own?

> **(There is) one Lord, one faith, one baptism, one God and Father of us all, who is above all and through all and in all.**
> **(Ephesians 4:5-6)**

> *Remind us, Father-Creator, that You made every living creature, every human being, and so we are sisters and brothers of each other.*

Lost in time

On a day when you haven't accomplished much, have you ever felt that you've just *lost* a day? On occasion, people have *really* lost days.

The Julian calendar, introduced in 46 B.C., was not exact, and lost a day every 128 years. Gradually, it got out of phase with the seasons.

So when the Gregorian calendar now used was adopted by much of Europe in 1582, there was a difference of 10 days. The days were just dropped. That year, the day following October 4 became October 15. Later, when the English adopted the Gregorian calendar, they lost 11 days.

Many of us "lose" time in a different sense — by procrastinating. Try to find time for things that truly matter to you and those you love.

You, beloved, are not in darkness, for that day to surprise you like a thief . . . let us not fall asleep as others do, but let us keep awake and be sober. (1 Thessalonians 5:4,6)

Indeed You have made us children of the light, Jesus. Therefore help us to keep alert.

The colors of the world

There are still people in this world, unfortunately, who do not accept others merely because of skin color. However, one company is helping our youngest generation see things in a new perspective.

Binney & Smith, the maker of Crayola crayons, has come out with new colors. They're called My World Colors and the box includes 16 skin, hair and eye colors including tan, black, mahogany, salmon and peach. The crayons help kids understand the many differences in real people. As a Binney & Smith spokesman put it, "Kids seem to have a good time trying to match the colors of the world around them."

People around the world are different — not only in skin color, but in religion, language and culture. If all of us learn to understand and accept the differences, we can fight ignorance and hatred.

> **Have we not all one father? Has not one God created us? Why then are we faithless to one another, profaning the covenant of our ancestors? (Malachi 2:10)**

> *That we might respect one another regardless of race, nationality, religion, ethnicity, class or culture, God and Father of us all.*

Two rings, one great difference

When Joe Theismann retired as quarterback for The Washington Redskins in 1985, he ended a record-setting career. But with it came some hard and unexpected lessons.

"I got stagnant," he says. "I thought the team revolved around me. . . . My approach had changed. I was griping about the weather, my shoes, practice times, everything.

"Today I wear my two rings — the winner's ring from Super Bowl XVII and the loser's ring from Super Bowl XVIII. The difference in those two rings lies in applying oneself and not accepting anything but the best."

There's nothing easy about always looking for the best in ourselves. But if we don't consider ourselves second-rate individuals, we owe it to ourselves to live up to our own highest standards.

Today, give life your best.

You shall love your neighbor as yourself. (Leviticus 19:18)

Jesus, enable me to love that person hardest to love, myself.

Give warmhearted recognition

If you think that commenting on the good in others will make them stuck-up, think again. According to writer Dr. Dale Turner, "There are those who have the curious impression that praising a person will make him conceited. Almost without exception the reverse is true. Few things are as humbling as warmhearted recognition and approval."

Try getting into the habit of letting people know when you appreciate their good deeds or good ideas. After all, each of us knows how wonderful it feels to have someone else remark sincerely on something we have accomplished.

As popular and famous as author Mark Twain was, he knew the value of encouraging words. He admitted, "I can live for two months on one good compliment."

So when someone compliments you — say thanks and enjoy it.

Putting away falsehood, let all of us speak the truth to our neighbors. (Ephesians 4:25)

Bless me with a truthful tongue, Jesus.

In moments of distress

Tim Rutten is a writer for the Los Angeles Times. One evening, while he was returning home with a pizza, he was accosted by two young men with guns. They robbed him of his wallet and his watch.

Then they pushed him face first into the ground and pointed their guns at his head. Rutten was sure that he was going to die. He remembers thinking about his wife and remembers praying, "Lord, have mercy on me, a sinner."

At that point, the muggers noticed the pizza. He told them to take it, and they left, without harming him any further.

In our times of distress, the Lord is there. Pray to Him and ask for the guidance, courage, and peace you need to get through. He will hear you.

If you . . . know how to give good gifts to your children, how much more will your Father . . . give good things to those who ask Him! (Matthew 7:11)

Generous Father, keep me ever mindful of the good things You are ever ready to give me.

Getting out of time traps

If you find that the only way to fit in all the tasks you have to do each day is to cut back on your sleep, you may be hurting both your health and your productivity.

Instead, Dale Hanson Bourke, author of "The Sleep Management Plan" makes these suggestions:

- Reduce the number of hours you watch television.
- Use your lunch hour once a week for a specific activity.
- Trade child-care activities with another parent.
- Make a priority list each day and do the important things first.
- Keep a log for a week and find places where you can reclaim wasted time.

Time's value is in how we use it and how we enjoy it. Take the time to thank God as well.

**For everything there is a season.
(Ecclesiastes 3:1)**

Show us how to order our time for our own eternal good and Your glory, Lord.

Offer help and understanding

Abortion is a painful topic upon which many people vehemently disagree. B. J. Issacson-Jones, the director of a St. Louis abortion clinic, and Andrew Puzder, a pro-life lawyer who helped write a Missouri law restricting abortion, are two of these people.

They were archenemies a few years ago, until they realized that they share a common ground — both have concerns about women and children. They have formed a controversial group of people who work together in areas they can agree on: adoption, foster care and abstinence for teenagers. Similar groups have formed in Texas and Massachusetts.

Believing that abortion is wrong and working against it is not enough. To be truly pro-life, each one of us needs to love each of God's children. Mothers and their babies need all the practical help and compassionate understanding they can get.

Be pro-life in every prayerful and constructive way you are able.

**Come . . . let us confer together.
(Nehemiah 6:7)**

Prince of Peace, enable people to discover areas of mutual agreement and build on them for the defense of every life.

Slow and easy does it

There's a world-wide hunt going on. It's not looking for treasure, but for the best idea on how to save the Leaning Tower of Pisa.

Since its construction over 800 years ago, it has gotten increasingly out of perpendicular — now, it leans about five-and-a-half yards.

So proposals are being sought to find the answer to stabilizing the problem. A couple of German experts recommend a system of computer-controlled hydraulic presses on concrete blocks around the foundation.

A Japanese plan suggests fitting the tower with a steel girdle and winching it back.

Whatever idea they finally choose will only bring the tower back about two feet — and only a fraction of an inch at a time.

For some problems, slow is best.

Abraham, having patiently endured, obtained the promise. (Hebrews 6:15)

Jesus, help us be careful and patient.

The case of the disappearing towns

Each year, as many as 200 towns in the United States just disappear from the map as far as the Postal Service is concerned.

When a small community's population dwindles, the local post office may close. Residents then receive their mail through the post office of another town.

The loss of their hometown mailing address can be a real blow to a community's sense of identity. But the residents still get their mail.

There are thousands of people who literally have no mailing address because they no longer have homes.

Through religious and community groups, we can reach out to these people. They need a sense of community as well as shelter.

See that none of you repays evil for evil, but always seek to do good.
(1 Thessalonians 5:15)

Compassionate Friend of humankind, how may we extend Your compassion to homeless persons?

Growing in wisdom

Here's some wisdom on aging from a woman who signs herself simply Angela.

According to her we must "find the balance between not fighting getting older and not giving in to getting older"; between our need for company and our need for solitude, because "balancing your needs successfully is the key to growing older with grace and dignity."

Angela continues, the "mistaken idea that we are no longer of use to anyone . . . does not lead to a graceful, dignified older age." And so she counsels, "do not waste one minute of your life living someone else's."

Angela sums up her wisdom by saying that "growing older with grace and dignity requires strength, courage, flexibility, patience, good humor, faith, and fortitude.

"We cannot fight or fool Mother Nature. The best we can do is embrace her."

After all, when we are older "life *is* still rich and full of meaning."

The fear of the Lord is the beginning of wisdom, and the knowledge of the Holy One is insight. (Proverbs 9:10)

Whatever its length, Wisdom of God, may my life be a song of praise and thanksgiving.

Speak the same language

The Chinese have no trouble communicating, even though ten major languages and dozens of minority languages are spoken in China.

Although an idea is expressed by different words in the many Chinese languages, it's written in the same symbols or ideograms in all of them. Everyone writes the same language.

In any nation, communication problems may occur between groups that "speak different languages" in the sense that their ethnic backgrounds are different.

But problems can often be resolved when groups realize that their basic values are the same.

There is no longer Greek and Jew, circumcised and uncircumcised, barbarian, Scythian, slave and free; but Christ is all and in all! (Colossians 3:11)

Source of our unity, Spirit of God, may we value what unites us, and minimize what divides us.

End trend of selfishness

James Lincoln Collier is a social historian. His book, "The Rise of Selfishness in America" offers some interesting perspectives on our values. He suggests that a trend toward selfishness began "as a reaction to the Victorian age, a time when there was a much stronger emphasis on community values. A great deal was wrong with the Victorian age, but people back then did have a very clear sense that you had duties to your fellow man.

"After World War I, people began feeling that they wanted to have a free, expressive life. Gradually, this became translated into a sense that we should feel good all the time. By the 1970s, this became an actual ethic that said you were wrong if you weren't putting yourself first."

Collier suggests that the only way to deal with today's problems is by paying attention to politics, the environment, and, especially, family life. That means making vital, selfless decisions.

Waywardness kills the simple, and the complacency of fools destroys them; but those who listen to (wisdom) will be secure. (Proverbs 1:32-33)

Come, Holy Spirit, come fill us with wisdom.

From riding to reading

Michael Anderer, 24, and Matthew Camuso, 23, are young men who have made a difference. The two friends rode their bicycles across the United States to raise awareness about the illiteracy problem in America.

Anderer and Camuso travelled from Seattle to Boston — a distance of 4,100 miles — in 42 days. Throughout the journey, they suffered from aching muscles, near dehydration, and occasionally getting lost. But the support and encouragement they received from strangers they met along the way kept them going.

Through sponsors, they raised $10,000 for the Literacy Volunteers of America. Their cross-country cycling trip will help some people learn how to read.

Each one of us has gifts and talents we can use to make a difference. What can *you* do to help others?

> **You are the body of Christ and individually members of it. And God has appointed in the church first apostles, second prophets, third teachers, then workers of miracles, then healers, helpers, administrators.**
> **(1 Corinthians 12:27-28)**

> *Alert me, Almighty God, to the gifts and talents You've graced me with for the common good.*

"Every creature prays"

Religion asks its adherents to pray either together or alone; in words or silently.

Even those who doubt God's existence may pray when they remark on the beauty of a human face, or of nature, for example.

Even "I cannot pray!" or "Why me?" can be prayers from the heart.

And according to an ancient Roman, Tertullian, "Every creature prays. Cattle and wild beasts pray . . . As they come from their barns and caves they look up to heaven and call out . . . in their own fashion.

"The birds . . . lift themselves up to heaven: they open out their wings . . . and give voice to what seems to be a prayer."

Tertullian concludes by saying, "What more need be said on the duty of prayer?"

What more indeed?

> **(Jesus) went out to the mountain to pray; and all night he continued in prayer to God. (Luke 6:12)**

Lord, teach us to pray as You would have us pray.

Keep trying to kick it

"People should never give up trying to stop drinking," says Igor Grant, chief psychiatrist at a University of California medical center.

Dr. Grant's recent study of alcoholics confirmed that those who quit drinking, even after years of addiction, can live as long as people who are only casual drinkers or nondrinkers.

Those alcoholics who stayed off alcohol during the period they were monitored (from one to eleven years), had a death rate the same as the general population the same age. Those who resumed drinking had a death rate five times as high.

Compulsive drinkers *can* kick the habit, no matter how entrenched it is. And by doing so, they can increase the quantity as well as the quality of their lives.

The word of God abides in you, and you have overcome the evil one. (1 John 2:14)

Strengthen me in my efforts to overcome whatever addictions and compulsions mar my freedom, Savior.

Sing out loud

If there is one activity that everyone seems to enjoy, it's singing. We sing in the car, the shower, at work or when we're home alone.

When we sing, we relax and enjoy ourselves. Experts have found that singing is good for you. It elevates the spirit, it helps to express thoughts and feelings, and it provides an emotional release. Humans are the only animal with a fully developed voice that can be used for speaking and singing.

From old-fashioned sing-alongs to the current popularity of karaoke machines — a device that allows you to sing with your favorite tunes — singing is an activity that brings different types of people together.

And remember when you are at church, don't be embarrassed to sing the hymns. Remember the old saying: "Those who sing pray twice."

Sing aloud to God our strength; shout for joy to the God of Jacob! Raise a song, sound the timbrel, the sweet lyre with the harp. (Psalm 81:1-2)

Jesus, give us the heart to sing — regardless of how we think we sound.

Good example from a good job

Almost any occupation can be used as a means of glorifying God.

Basketball player Horace Grant of the Chicago Bulls said, "The Lord gave Moses a rod to perform miracles. He gave Samson the jawbone of a donkey, and I believe He has given me a basketball to use to glorify Him."

People in sports have a special chance to glorify God by serving as positive role models for young people.

But whatever your occupation, there are always opportunities to set a good example. Whatever you do that is a positive, constructive influence on others is also a service to God.

Let your light shine before others, so that they may see your good works and give glory to your Father in heaven. (Matthew 5:16)

Holy Spirit, enable the lamp of my life to burn brightly today.

The gift of hope

At a time when political and economic conditions in Czechoslovakia must have been pretty discouraging, the nation's president, Vaclav Havel, said in a speech:

"I . . . carry hope in my heart. Hope is a feeling that life and work have meaning. You either have it or you don't, regardless of the state of the world around you. Life without hope is an empty, boring, and useless life. I cannot imagine that I could strive for something if I did not carry hope in me. I am thankful to God for this gift. It is as big a gift as life itself."

When we, like Vaclav Havel, find ourselves in difficult circumstances, our hope can sustain us — the hope that comes from knowing that life has meaning, that God loves us and is always with us.

God so loved the world that He gave His only Son, so that everyone who believes in Him may not perish but may have eternal life. (John 3:16)

Thank You, Father, for the gift of Your Son.

Breaking the cycle of violence

When it comes to the problem of domestic violence, the news isn't good.

"As many as 35 percent of women who visit hospital emergency departments do so for symptoms related to continuing physical abuse," reports American Medical News. The paper continues, "Family violence is the single largest cause of injury to women in this country."

And Dr. Antonia Novello, the United States Surgeon General, adds: "Violence against women by their intimate partners is responsible for more injuries than car crashes, rape, and muggings combined."

If you or someone you know is battered, get help. Whether from shelters, hospitals or the police, seek assistance from professionals. Remember that you are not to blame for the violent actions of another. And there is hope if you look for it.

Cast all your anxiety on (God), because He cares for you. (1 Peter 5:7)

Jesus, enable me to trust You so much that indeed I cast all my cares on You.

Curtain's up — again

Back in 1970, Dorothy Mavrich may not have been the only person in Joliet, Illinois, to regret that the beautiful old Rialto Square Theatre was slated to be demolished. But she was the only one who decided to fight to preserve it.

For years she campaigned, speaking up at public meetings, gradually coaxing others into volunteering their efforts to save the historic theatre. In time the building was bought, funds were raised for renovation, and performances begun once again.

More than that, the Rialto has been the centerpiece for the redevelopment of the entire city center. Over a million people have seen the curtain raised on the stage that was once destined to be turned into a parking lot.

Dorothy Mavrich had a goal and the determination and courage to reach it.

**You are the light of the world.
(Matthew 5:14)**

Light the candle of my life with Your grace, Lord of all hopefulness.

To become young

When Pablo Picasso was 85, he was asked why his *later* paintings were more innovative than his *early* ones. How could the *later* paintings have more of the boldness and fire of a *young* artist's work?

Picasso's reply was, "It takes a long time to become young."

To him, the years didn't bring a loss of creativity or enthusiasm. They brought exciting new ideas and insights and opportunities.

Such an outlook is an inspiration to others.

In his book "Life in the Afternoon," Edward Fischer says, "Your attitude in old age is a form of inheritance, something handed on to those you meet along the road. If you hand on encouragement of spirit, that will be a more valuable heirloom than graspable objects."

> **O God, from my youth you have taught me . . . so even to old age and gray hairs, O God, do not forsake me. (Psalm 71:17,18)**

Ancient of Days, be with Your aged daughters and sons and comfort them.

For babies: sew much love

Maureen McCormack has seven children of her own, but she still has time to head a Brooklyn group of the organization called ABC Quilts.

ABC Quilts was founded by a New Hampshire grandmother to make quilts for babies with AIDS or who are HIV positive, as well as for those born to drug or alcohol addicted parents, or who were abandoned by their parents. It's now become a national organization.

Mrs. McCormack's Brooklyn group alone has distributed 9,000 quilts. Many individuals and organizations help make the quilts — from retired people to schoolchildren. Youngsters help decorate quilt squares with fabric markers, often including little messages like "I love you."

These folks, like countless other volunteers, find their work a labor of love.

Help these women, for they have labored side by side . . . in the gospel. (Philippians 4:3)

Inspire our efforts to ease the suffering of those with AIDS or AIDS-related complex, Divine Physician.

All God's creation

I'd like to share this thought-provoking poem with you.

"I was hungry and you fed me; / Thirsty and you gave me to drink. / Cold and you gave me a blanket; / Lonely and you opened your heart./ Wagging my tail I trotted in / With nothing but my love to give. / Now I am yours and you are mine; / And I think that sometimes you too / See in your dreams the face of One / Who said 'Care for one of these / And you will also care for Me!' "

Yes, the speaker is a stray dog. But did you ever consider this: the way you treat any part of Creation is an indication of the way you treat yourself and your fellow human beings?

Tenderheartedness begins with the smallest part of Creation. Respect for them is respect for their Creator and ours.

God said, 'Let the waters bring forth swarms of living creatures, and let birds fly . . . Let the earth bring forth living creatures.' (Genesis 1:20,24)

Let us respect the smallest part of Creation and so respect the Creator of everything.

The strains of work

All of us have had bad days at work. Problems on the job can stem from anything like an uncooperative co-worker, a bad business deal, or a mean boss. If these situations build up, they can cause stress, poor job performance, and low self-esteem.

There are ways to handle these work-related predicaments. Social scientist Albert Mehrabian of UCLA suggests that you establish a presence. When you project confidence in your body language and voice, you command respect.

Avoid arguments and outbursts in front of a group. Instead, identify your most common trouble areas and try to get to the root of the problem.

Creative solutions to simple problems will make your work environment a happier, healthier place.

Those with good sense are slow to anger, and it is to their glory to overlook an offense . . . A violent tempered person will pay the penalty. (Proverbs 19:11,19)

While anger is a normal emotion, Creator, it does need to be directed and channeled. Show me how to do that in a wholesome way.

One woman's long life

Most of us take for granted the comforts and luxuries that we have in the nineties — cars, TV's, computers, compact disc players and such. Marie Graves remembers when none of these things existed. That's because she recently celebrated her 100th birthday.

Mrs. Graves has 2 children, 4 grandchildren, 8 great-grandchildren, and 4 great-great-grandchildren. She is known around her community near Sioux City, Iowa, for her zest for life. When asked to what she attributes her long and happy life, she replied: "Living a clean life, having wonderful parents who guided me in the ways of the Lord, my quest to continue learning new things and my faith in God."

Marie Graves has her life in perspective. Two of the main ingredients in a happy, healthy life are family and faith. Where do they fit into your life?

The steadfast love of the Lord is . . . on those who fear Him . . . (on) those who keep His covenant and remember to do His commandments. (Psalm 103:17,18)

Lord God, help me walk in the way of Your covenant, and so do my part to nourish my faith and family.

New dimensions in junk food

A headline some months ago read: "All the News That's Fit to Eat."

The article that followed described how old newspapers can now be fed to cattle. A professor of animal nutrition at the University of Illinois has found a way to treat shredded newspapers so that sheep and cattle can digest the cellulose in them. The paper, it seems, contains a lot of glucose, and the animals gobble up the treated paper. But it has little vitamin or mineral content.

The same might be said of much of the fare provided by the media, especially TV. Lots of it decidedly falls into the "junk food" category.

But there are also many programs of real value. Parents and teachers can help young people become discerning in their TV viewing.

> **I prayed, and understanding was given me; I called upon God and the spirit of wisdom came to me. (Wisdom of Solomon 7:7)**

Come, Spirit of Counsel, come!

Positive point of view

A journalist commented in amazement that actor Bruce Adler never seems to complain.

Adler replied: "My grandmother used to say some people complain because they have no shoes, other people complain because they have no feet." He added, "I just have no shoelaces."

Adler's view of acting is certainly positive. He loves it. To him, success means "going to the theater and making people laugh." He's now making them laugh in the Broadway musical "Crazy for You."

For two years in a row, he's been nominated for a Tony Award for the best featured actor in a musical — and lost. But far from complaining, he talks about how great it is to be nominated.

Keeping a positive outlook lets us experience the joy of living.

Always continue in the fear of the Lord. Surely there is a future, and your hope will not be cut off. (Proverbs 23:17-18)

May my loving obedience to You, Lord God, be the source of my hope for a better future.

All in good fun

Literary fans know Stephen King, Amy Tan, Dave Barry, Roy Blount, Jr., and Dave Marsh as talented authors. During a recent American Booksellers Association convention, however, they and other writers showed off their musical skills by performing as the band, The Rock Bottom Remainders.

The group performed popular tunes from the 60's and 70's to a full house of publishers and book dealers. Their musical efforts helped raise $15,000 for three charities. It also provided a good time for both the audience and the band members. Stephen King described it as "liberating."

These professional writers have given us all an example of how we can let loose once in a while and just have fun. A sense of humor is essential for a happy and successful life.

(God) made them rejoice with great joy. (Nehemiah 12:43)

Jesus, make us joyous.

Won't you be my valentine?

Let me introduce some of life's greatest lovers. These folks were recognized by *Good Housekeeping* magazine for their contributions.

All 17,000 Doctors with a Heart serve their poor and uninsured patients on Valentine's Day without charge.

A Sunday-school class helps financially pressed farmers sell their crops.

A Colorado group makes teddy bears for local police and fire fighters to give to traumatized children.

A radio producer writes news summaries and reads them to the blind.

A paralegal goes to court with abused women, helps with the paper work, gives them moral support.

A hairdresser charges residents of a homeless shelter "a smile" for a haircut.

Love is for giving, not just for receiving. How can you give the gift of love?

Consider how to stir up one another to love and good works. (Hebrews 10:24)

Jesus, how may I love You more dearly through love of family members, friends, neighbors, self?

One-of-a-kind proposal

Roland Nadon and Marissa Massegnan were visiting Universal Studios in California when a director approached them. He said he needed two people to tape a wedding commercial for the amusement park. The couple agreed to do it. Towards the end of the taping, the would-be groom offered the would-be bride an engagement ring and asked her to marry him.

She was confused because the ring looked like one that she had picked out a year before. It turned out that it was the ring. Her fiance had arranged the entire thing as a unique way to propose.

In this busy world, it's not always easy to take the time to show our loved ones how much we care. Take the time and think of special ways to express yourself.

> **I pledged Myself to you and entered into a covenant with you, says the Lord God, and you became Mine. (Ezekiel 16:8)**

> *May my love for You imitate Your faithful love, Lord of the Covenant.*

Loved and loving 'til the end

Suzy Eldridge was a pre-school teacher who was known as "Miss Suzy" to all the children who loved her. She enjoyed playing with the youngsters, giving them silly nicknames and making them laugh.

Suzy Eldridge died from AIDS at the age of 29. She had continued to teach throughout her illness. Her funeral was attended by many family, friends, and students — people who had not let AIDS get in the way of their love. The kids were not afraid of AIDS — they were more worried that they would make her sick if they visited her when they had colds. As one fellow teacher and friend put it, "We were more of a threat to her than she was to us."

It's a fact that you can't catch AIDS from hugging or other casual contact. Rather than judge people who have AIDS, offer them your compassion. They need it.

> **Do not judge, so that you may not be judged. For with the judgment you make you will be judged and the measure you give will be the measure you get. (Matthew 7:1)**

Holy Spirit, help me be non-judgmental.

Feasting, fasting and Lent

Here are some suggestions for a wholesome Lent from writer Jeanette Martino Land:

- Fast from criticism, feast on praise.
- Fast from self-pity, feast on joy.
- Fast from ill temper, feast on peace.
- Fast from resentment, feast on contentment.
- Fast from jealousy, feast on love.
- Fast from pride, feast on humility.
- Fast from selfishness, feast on service.
- Fast from fear, feast on trust in God.

On second thought, these could be suggestions for a wholesome life year-round.

A wholesome life is a God-centered life which struggles to put aside what in our nature is against the Supreme Law, which is love of God and love of neighbor as one's self.

Sacrifice and offering You do not desire; but You have given me an open ear . . . I delight to do Your will, O my God. (Psalm 40:6,8)

May my life be one of listening to Your call to justice and mercy, Merciful One.

Young fathers

A group of young men met in Manhattan recently to discuss the subject of diapers.

They were the Manhattan Valley Teen Fathering group — young fathers who meet every week to talk about subjects ranging from finances to teething.

Until recently, there were few support groups for fathers. But many young men evidently need help coping with the problems of parenthood.

"If you have a lot of friends who don't have children, you really can't talk to them about children," says 19-year-old Felix Figueroa. "But here . . . you feel less alone."

Reaching out to others so that we are "less alone," is part of being just plain human.

One must help the weak, remembering the words of the Lord Jesus . . . 'It is more blessed to give than to receive.' (Acts 20:35)

Merciful Savior, show us how to "help the weak," instruct the ignorant, counsel the doubtful and calm the troubled.

Dream becomes real

Jean Forman had wanted to be a doctor for as long as she could remember. But she had put off college to start a family.

She decided to enroll in college at age 40. With some encouragement from her family, she graduated from the University of Southern California School of Medicine at the age of 51, becoming the oldest student to earn a degree from the school.

Dr. Forman plans on becoming a family physician. She said, "We each have one lifetime to do something with. Even if I had not made it to medical school, at least I would know that I tried. If I had not, I would have always wondered, 'What if?' "

We all have goals and dreams that we can accomplish with some effort. Work on making *your* dream a reality.

Your sons and your daughters shall prophesy . . . dream dreams, and . . . see visions. (Joel 2:28)

Lord of the prophetesses and prophets of every age, fill us with Your Spirit.

On rootlessness and mobility

Rootlessness means being fancy free and not tied to any one place or person. Not caring about any little patch of ground. Able to move on anytime, for any reason.

And mobility — not just so-called upward mobility, but changing houses, schools, religions, political party affiliation means moving on, staying free.

But writer and farmer Stanley Crawford takes exception to these two common American traits. Speaking of his hometown, Dixon, California, Crawford says, ". . . being rooted, embedded, connected with a place . . . can be difficult, painful, claustrophobic at times. But I can't see a future in which we all buzz around as much as we do now . . . This place is what I am, is my work."

Where's your place . . . your roots?

The Lord will inherit Judah as His portion in the holy land, and will again choose Jerusalem. Be silent, all people, before the Lord. (Zechariah 2:12-13)

May we put down deep roots into the holy land in which You've planted us, Creator.

Parents, children and acceptance

Do you want to have a reasonably happy home? Then try these six suggestions from Linda and Michael Courtney, writing in "Marriage Partnership."

● As long as nothing's dead or dying in a child's room, they needn't keep it clean once they are past ten.

● It's OK to get one's shoes wet having fun.

● Mistakes are okay, too.

● So long as they're not failing in school, it is really all right for children to escape into an occasional sitcom or other TV show.

● Children "need to learn to practice expressing feelings in a safe way that does not harm others or lead to rejection."

● "Children need an oasis" where they can be children, and be sure that "they are an important part of" their parents' lives.

Children *are* God's gift to their parents.

(Children) are indeed a heritage from the Lord. (Psalm 127:3)

Father, enable parents to see their children as Your gift to them.

Encouragement for education

Ewing Kauffman is a successful businessman who's concerned about education for today's youth. He started a program in a high school in Kansas City, Missouri, called Project Choice. The program is an incentive for students to finish high school.

The students who graduate from Westport High School will receive financial support from Mr. Kauffman for college, vocational school, or on-the-job training. The program also provides services such as workshops, tutoring, and college board preparation classes. Since Project Choice began, the percentage of college-bound seniors has risen from 20 to 70 percent.

Ewing Kauffman is a man who cares about where our future is headed. If there are students in your life, try to help them out by encouraging them in any way you can.

Those who are wise shall shine like the brightness of the sky, and those who lead the many to righteousness, like the stars forever. (Daniel 12:3)

Bless all who teach through word and deed, Divine Teacher.

The face of courage

It's not often that anyone willingly gives up a bright political career for the principles of personal conscience. The Profile in Courage Award bestowed by the Kennedy Foundation to reward "bravery in politics" selected a man who did just that.

Charles Weltner was a Georgia representative in 1966. Weltner needed to sign a loyalty oath which would have meant supporting avowed segregationist Lester Maddox in the race for governor. He declined and by not seeking re-election he gave up his plans for a political future. He returned to private legal practice, and later became a Georgia Supreme Court Justice.

Charles Weltner's attitude is expressed in a quote from Vaclav Havel that he keeps on his desk: "I simply take the side of truth against any lie, of sense against nonsense, justice against injustice."

Seek good, and not evil. (Amos 5:14)

Redeemer, show me how to be just in all my dealings, with others, with self.

Time out for prayer

How many times have you and I heard that we must pray, we ought to pray, that prayer can change us and change the world?

But how do we pray in a meaningful way in today's hectic world?

Writing in Fellowship in Prayer magazine, P. H. Raynis suggests:

● that we use a prayer calendar noting people and intentions that need each day's prayers;

● that we pray about the troubling events in our newspapers and magazines;

● that we adopt an influential person, or a troubled person or nation spiritually by praying for them daily;

● that we join a prayer group;

● or that we begin a prayer network of our own.

Prayer is the most important activity we can do; and the most flexible. Adapt prayer to your life-style.

Lord, teach us to pray. (Luke 11:1)

Yes, Lord Jesus, teach us to pray in the way uniquely suited to our life-styles and personalities.

Sniffing out unusual gift

If you think you don't have any special abilities, you're probably overlooking them. They're not all as obvious as musical talent.

One of Richard Duffee's special gifts is a well-developed sense of smell, which he's made the basis of a successful career.

He works as an "odor detective," tracking down the sources of unpleasant odors — and neutralizing them. Some sources, like fish canneries and sewage-treatment plants, are easy to spot. Others are hard to trace.

Duffee has his own company, Odor Science and Engineering. His clients include research labs, corporations, and environmental consulting firms.

Our special gifts take many forms. All are important if we use them well.

**There are varieties of gifts.
(1 Corinthians 12:4)**

How can I use the special gifts You've given me, Counselor?

Eaten away by corrosion

Books printed before the middle of the 19th century endured many hundreds of years. Today's books self-destruct after fifty years or so.

The reason is changes in papermaking. Chemicals now used in the process leave an acid residue that gradually eats away the paper.

In our lives, there's an equally corrosive effect when we harbor anger and resentment. Holding a grudge against someone who has wronged us destroys our physical, emotional, and spiritual well-being.

There are times when it's natural to feel anger or resentment, but we can get rid of them through forgiveness. Forgiveness not only frees others from the destructive effect of our ill will, it frees us as well.

> **Peter (asked) . . . 'how often should I forgive? As many as seven times?' Jesus said to him, 'Not seven times, but . . . seventy-seven times.' (Matthew 18:21-22)**

Forgiving Lord, enable me to forgive, also.

Donating life

If you have ever thought about donating blood but had some questions about your safety or eligibility, here are some answers from the Puget Sound Blood Program.

First, you cannot get AIDS or any other disease by giving blood. Only sterile, disposable needles and equipment are used so you will not be at risk.

Your plasma is restored in only 24 hours. Your red blood cells will replace themselves in two to four weeks. If you are 18 years old, weigh at least 110 pounds and are in good health, you can donate as often as every two months.

And who will benefit? People with cancer, with heart, blood vessel and gastrointestinal diseases, or those who face emergencies like car accidents or burns need your help.

Decide to be a life-saver.

Is it lawful to do good or to do harm on the sabbath, to save life or to kill? (Mark 3:4)

Lord of life, how can we save life?

Caring is catching on

A Norwalk, Connecticut, mother was concerned because the hallways of her son's high school were dingy and unattractive. Budget cuts made it impossible for the school to paint them. But Nan Haavik refused to believe it couldn't be done.

She organized parents to paint the halls. Since union regulations didn't allow volunteers to do maintenance painting, the parents made the paint job decorative — adding sports, art, and music symbols along the walls. They worked during team and band practice to avoid the cost of keeping the building open after hours.

Now the number of volunteers has grown and the school is getting a thorough refurbishing.

Mrs. Haavik says, "I just try to . . . show the world somebody cares. It's contagious."

A man was going down from Jerusalem to Jericho, and he fell among robbers . . . but a Samaritan . . . came to where he was; and . . . had compassion. (Luke 10:30,33)

I pray that I might be compassionate, God.

Promise and silence of Lent

The word "Lent" comes from an Old English word for "Spring," and rightly so, for these seasons coincide.

Writing about that coincidence Thomas Merton said, "The woods have all become young in the discipline of spring: but it is the discipline of expectancy only. There are no buds . . . the wilderness shines with promise. The land is dressed in simplicity and strength. Everything foretells the coming of the holy spring . . . woods, hills, birds, water, and sky . . . remained mute in the presence of the Beloved."

Centuries before, Zechariah had written "The Lord will inherit Judah as His portion in the holy land . . . Be silent, all people, before (Him)."

I wonder, do we keep Lent as a time of silent expectancy for "the Beloved"?

> **The Lord is in His holy temple; let all the earth keep silence before Him.**
> **(Habakkuk 2:20)**

Teach me to be silent before You, O Lord, even in the midst of work or play.

Crime fighter and bridge-builder

Felice Kirby has her own way of fighting crime. First she meets with a block association or other neighborhood group to identify the sources of area crime.

Then she meets with local police to learn what they consider to be the sources of crime in the area.

Usually there's some agreement between citizens and police. So Ms. Kirby of the Citizens' Committee for New York City helps them meet, set goals and plan ways to reach those goals to eliminate the agreed-upon sources of crime.

Her own goals, Ms. Kirby says, are to show the police that the local "community (is) a resource instead of a problem." And to show the local community that the police "are able to accomplish things."

Felice Kirby is a bridge-builder. She makes communication possible between groups that are sometimes suspicious of each other.

Bridge-building is possible. So is communication and peace.

Blessed are the peacemakers, for they will be called children of God. (Matthew 5:9)

Dear Prince of Peace, enable us to be peacemakers.

Balancing act for young workers

Many young people — and their parents — think that it's good for teens to have part-time jobs. It can mean earning money as well as learning responsibility. That's true. But only up to a point.

The fact is that too much work can interfere with schoolwork and home life. Dr. John Stephenson of the University of Wisconsin Hospital recommends that parents set rules that school marks stay up. Moms and dads should also limit work time to no more than 16 hours a week. And, for safety's sake, they should check working conditions for their youngsters.

Most people want to earn their own way, to be productive. But work is still only one part of life. We need to keep a balance for our own health and well-being.

And that's a job for a whole lifetime.

A sabbath rest still remains for the people of God; for those who enter God's rest also cease from their labors as God did. (Hebrews 4:8-10)

Lord of the Sabbath, show us how to enter into Your rest.

Reading: your gift to give

Imagine how it would feel to live in a country where you couldn't read the language — say in China. Street signs would be meaningless. You wouldn't be able to read labels on food packages or instructions for using appliances.

Many people in our country are handicapped in this way because they can't read their *own* language. They are often so embarrassed about their problem that they conceal it instead of trying to remedy it. But they constantly have to ask for directions and may have trouble at work.

Lots of communities have tutoring programs or reading classes for adults. If you know someone who seems to have a reading problem, check on programs available and tactfully let the person know. You'll be giving him or her a precious gift.

> **Jesus said to (Bartimaeus), 'What do you want Me to do for you?' And the blind man said to Him, 'Master, let me receive my sight.' And Jesus said to him, 'Go your way; your faith has made you well.'**
> **(Mark 10:51-52)**

May we help others to see You in us, Lord God.

Waking up to life

As we get older, we tend to sleep less soundly. Doctors say this is no cause for alarm. What *is* cause for alarm is habitual use of sleeping pills. They often cause side effects like anxiety and confusion — problems that can make elderly people appear senile. As a result, they may be sent to nursing homes unnecessarily.

Dr. Marshall Folstein of Johns Hopkins University School of Medicine thinks older people's use of sleeping pills is often caused by boredom. He says, "The real problem is, they don't have anything to do when they're awake, so they want to be asleep."

It's important to remain active in your interests, even if you have to slow down physically. You may have to retire from your job, but you don't have to retire from life.

Awake, O sleeper . . . and Christ shall give you light. (Ephesians 5:14)

Rouse the retired from the sleep of non-involvement, God.

Responsibility to God's world

One of the hot topics of the day is the environment. But the many issues and problems won't be easily or quickly resolved. Brenda Peterson, writing in "Nature and Other Mothers," says that the unique perspectives of men and women can work together for the good of the earth.

"For years environmentalists have been educating us to recognize that the whole wide world is our home; we cannot leave the world, or transcend it, or truly throw anything away. We must learn to be here. If women claim the world the way they already have their homes and if men claim their homes as fervently as they have the world, what might we create?"

It's a good question. All God's children have the responsibility and the opportunity to keep our home planet, and even beyond, healthy for now and into the future.

Ask yourself what you can do today.

The Lord answered Job out of the whirlwind . . . 'Where were you when I laid the foundation of the earth?' (Job 38:1,4)

Creator, enable me to appreciate the earth which You formed and set in place as my home.

Rekindling light and warmth

You may have seen the sort of trick birthday candles that relight when they are blown out. These novelty candles have wicks treated with magnesium crystals. The wicks retain heat so well that they rekindle themselves as soon as they are blown out.

These unquenchable little candles bring to mind the joy that comes from trusting God.

It's a joy that can't be extinguished by our circumstances. When others wrong us, we forgive them because we know that we, too, do wrong and need forgiveness. In times of trouble, or illness, or the death of a loved one, we don't despair, for we know that God is with us.

A joyful heart retains the warmth of God's love and is perpetually rekindled by it.

**My times are in Your hand; deliver me . . . save me in Your steadfast love.
(Psalm 31:15,16)**

Father, I put my life in Your hands.

"Live to give, not get"

Letitia Baldridge is a world respected expert on manners and etiquette. She has some advice to offer people who would like to make new friends.

To be the kind of person that others want to be around takes a winning personality. Just what does that mean? Miss Baldridge says it's a matter of how you "project inner beauty, goodness and giving."

If that sounds like a cliche, think again. After all, "the most loved people live to give, not get. Make others feel good about themselves and they will feel good about you." Don't worry about people reciprocating.

Instead, "on meeting someone, think, 'what does he or she need to feel good?' and fulfill the need as much as you can."

We human beings all need one another in ways large and small. And always, we need kindness.

> Love your enemies and pray for those who persecute you, so that you may be children of your Father in heaven. (Matthew 5:44-45)

Merciful Savior, imbue me with Your own mercy.

Open the way to creativity

The animated cartoon characters created by Chuck Jones have been making children — and adults — laugh for the past 60 years. Bugs Bunny, Porky Pig, and Daffy Duck are among his popular characters.

Where does Jones get his ideas? When he was asked about his creativity, he said, "You can't force inspiration. It's like trying to catch a butterfly with a hoop but no net. If you keep your mind open and receptive, though, one day a butterfly will land on your finger."

We tend to associate creativity with the arts, but it's just as much a part of everyday life. Gardening can be creative. So can cooking, or organizing a group, or planning a trip.

Be open to new ideas and ways of doing things and you'll be surprised at your own creativity.

I waited patiently for the Lord. (Psalm 40:1)

Through patient and attentive waiting on Your inspiration, Lord, make my whole life creative.

Making sense of cents

Most people don't consider pennies as anything but a nuisance. They have a way of gathering at the bottoms of our pockets and purses. But thanks to one man, pennies are helping people in need.

Louis Sensel of Covington, Kentucky, started by setting up a "penny pot" in his community. People toss their unwanted pennies into the pot and the money gathered from it is used to buy food for the needy at Christmas. The first year, they raised $200. Most recently, they raised $450 — enough to provide food baskets for 42 families.

Louis Sensel has proved that just a little effort can help many people. Try to do something that will help others in your community.

Encourage one another and build up each other. (1 Thessalonians 5:11)

Man from Nazareth, what can I do to help others in my community?

Sweet silence

Solitude and silence have all but been elimi-
nated from our lives. Yet silence and solitude are
a holy acknowledgement of a center within the
self that can be creativity's fertile ground, a sanc-
tuary for self-observation.

Poet Margaret Gibson has written, "You don't
have to journey to a place (apart) . . . to discover
the silence within you." You can build silence into the ordinariness of your days.

Explain your need for silence to those you live
with; schedule your silent times and decide how
to spend them; notice what interferes with your
silence; then prepare for the creativity that often
comes.

Mostly, though, enjoy the psychological, spiritual and physical rest silence brings. And thank
God for this sweet gift.

**In returning and rest you shall be saved; in
quietness and in trust shall be your strength.
(Isaiah 30:15)**

*Holy Spirit, lead us to that silent oasis within
ourselves.*

Seeking excellence

When Mark Kator was called on to start the first long-term medical center for AIDS patients, he knew it wouldn't be an easy task. The first thing he had to do was calm the fears of his own staff.

Now Coler Memorial Hospital in New York is able to offer services from lab tests to dental care for the AIDS patients who come there. And Mr. Kator has won the respect of his workers as well as the sick people who depend on their help.

Mr. Kator admits that "there is always a challenge around the corner in health care." But he finds his greatest satisfaction in "being able to provide important services to people in need and to try to do it excellently."

Doing our jobs not just adequately but excellently can be tough. But it can also mean the sense of fulfillment that comes with true success.

> **Know well the condition of your flocks, and give attention to your herds; for riches do not last forever. (Proverbs 27:23)**

> *Enable me to be as attentive to detail as You are, Creator and Sustainer.*

Humor to lift the heart

Humor, like most anything else, can be destructive when it's misused, when it belittles or ridicules others.

So called "funny" novelty items are often designed to embarrass or cause discomfort to others. The owner of a novelty shop in San Francisco says, "If it smells bad, causes or simulates pain, or makes fun of someone, it will sell."

A coughing ashtray may be a harmless trick item, but a mirror that laughs when you look into it is about as funny as sneezing powder. Such tricks are insensitive, if not cruel.

Humor at its best lifts our hearts and draws us closer together. It makes us laugh *with* others, not *at* them.

> **Our mouth was filled with laughter, and our tongue with shouts of joy . . . The Lord has done great things. (Psalm 126:2,3)**

Put a laugh in my mouth, joy in my heart, Mirthful Lord.

An important role model

Students consider Julius Morgan a benevolent despot. The principal of Louis Brandeis High School says simply, "Julius does everything."

For over a quarter of a century, Julius Morgan has been assistant custodian at the building — and much more.

In addition to keeping the classrooms and grounds in good repair, he takes an interest in everybody and everything. He has donated equipment and trophies to the various sports teams. Julius Morgan wants each student to take advantage of every opportunity to learn and to have fun.

He says, "You have to be a role model to kids. They need somebody to talk to. I respect them and they respect me."

Respect and kindness make a world of difference.

Little children, let us love . . . in truth and action. (1 John 3:18)

Teach me to love as You love, Holy One.

Art of self-restraint

We often speak of acting out of thoughtfulness and kindness. But, sometimes it's just as essential not to act too quickly.

Arthur Conan Doyle, author of the Sherlock Holmes tales, recounted this incident from his friendship with writer George Meredith: "The nervous complaint from which he suffered caused him to fall down occasionally. As we walked up the narrow path I heard him fall behind me, but judged from the sound that it was a mere slither and could not have hurt him. Therefore I walked on as if I had heard nothing. He was a fiercely proud old man and my instincts told me that his humiliation in being helped would be far greater than any relief I could give him."

It's hard to restrain ourselves when our first reaction is to do something. Sometimes, the best thing to do is nothing.

> **(The) commandments . . . are summed up in this sentence, 'You shall love your neighbor as yourself.' Love does no wrong to a neighbor; therefore love is the fulfilling of the law. (Romans 13:9-10)**

> *Holy Spirit, how may I be tactful and charitable at the same time?*

Troubled family has good neighbors

An emotionally disabled family — two sisters and a brother — were about to lose their home in Huntington Station, Long Island, because they'd failed to pay their property taxes.

Then people from the area learned about their plight and came to the rescue.

One couple donated $20,000 toward a trust fund to pay the taxes. A woman who works at two jobs found time to organize a fund-raising dinner. A lawyer represented them without charge. A contractor offered to repair their house. And a county legislator began work on legislation to protect other emotionally disturbed people who can't handle business matters.

Concerned neighbors saved this family from being out on the streets. Transform your concern into action.

> **When you give alms, do not let your left hand know what your right hand is doing. (Matthew 6:3)**

> *When I give alms, Father, help me to do it quietly, mindful of the feelings of those I'm helping.*

Courtesy, technologically speaking

The widespread use of electronic gadgets has created new problems in telephone etiquette.

Answering machines have been called the modern equivalent of the butler. Part of a butler's job was to answer the phone briefly and courteously and take a message. He didn't force a caller to listen while he sang or performed comedy routines.

Call-waiting devices now permit you to interrupt a phone conversation and keep one person waiting indefinitely while you talk to another. But courtesy *doesn't* permit it.

And portable cellular phones obviously don't belong at places like theaters or restaurants.

Technology may change, but basic courtesy doesn't. It's simply consideration for others.

Let us love one another. (2 John, 5)

Enable me to express my love for others by my courtesy, gracious God.

Knowing our place in the universe

These days more and more of us are considering the environment and our place in it. We are asking about our responsibilities, about what we can do and where we fit in.

I'd like to share with you the words of a 16th century Irish cleric who saw himself as part of the universe, even as he prayed for his own soul.

Holy God, he prayed: "I entreat Thee by water . . . I entreat Thee by earth . . . I entreat Thee by every living creature that ever tasted death and life. I entreat Thee by time with its clear divisions, I entreat Thee by darkness, I entreat Thee by the light. I entreat all the elements in heaven and earth. That the eternal sweetness may be granted to my soul."

God wants us to enjoy the fruits of His creation. But He also asks for our wisdom and care.

Long ago You laid the foundation of the earth; and the heavens are the work of Your hands. (Psalm 102:25)

Remind us, Creator, that we are only stewards of what You created — the earth, its resources and all its creatures.

Building shelters of hope

A group of teenagers in Shoreview, Minnesota, learned a lot when they served dinner at a shelter for the homeless. A letter of thanks from one of the homeless people made a real impression.

The letter not only thanked the young people, it also urged them to avoid the causes of homelessness. The main causes given were lack of education, drug or alcohol addiction, and estrangement from family and friends.

In our efforts to help those who are homeless, we mustn't lose sight of underlying problems and needs. Some homeless people need job training. Others need treatment at drug rehabilitation centers, or need psychiatric help. And all need the moral support of being part of a group.

The homeless need more than just shelter.

(Jesus) saw a great crowd; and He had compassion for them, because they were like sheep without a shepherd. (Mark 6:34)

Jesus, how can I extend Your compassion to the sick homeless?

Turning a foreign phrase

If you have the chance to travel in foreign countries, one of the problems — and delights — of hearing other languages is interpreting idioms. Just as in English, we say "It's raining cats and dogs," in France it comes down in ropes; in Spain, in jugs; and in Italy, water basins.

Every language has its own wonderful way with words. French seems especially preoccupied with food and drink. The equivalent of turning up like a bad penny is arriving like a hair in the soup. We might say knee-high to a grasshopper. In France the comparison is as tall as three apples.

Throughout history, people have transformed language into something of charm and beauty. Unfortunately, words are also capable of causing great harm.

Try to speak the way you'd like to be spoken to.

Whoever listens to you listens to Me. (Luke 10:16)

Let us remember, Jesus, that our voices are the ones others hear.

Staying flexible

It's long been a source of amazement that a tree can often survive a hurricane that destroys buildings around it.

Scientists explain that because a building has greater surface area, it offers more resistance than the tree and is subjected to greater wind pressure. And the tree turns and bends with the wind, avoiding much of its force.

During a crisis in our lives, we, too, need to remain flexible. We should be willing to consider new options. For instance, if we are unhappy with a job, we can be open to trying another field.

Flexibility in our outlook could mean a more satisfying outcome.

The wind blows where it wills, and you hear the sound of it, but you do not know whence it comes or whither it goes; so it is with every one who is born of the Spirit. (John 3:8)

Open my ears to hear and my whole being to follow Your inspirations, Spirit of God.

A springtime harmony

The flowering of the woods in spring may seem haphazard, with each plant just doing its own thing. But botanists tell us the process is as carefully orchestrated as a symphony.

Flowers appear first on the small plants near the ground. These always bloom early, before the taller plants above them put out flowers and leaves — and shut out the sun.

Then in orderly succession, buds next unfurl on the shrubs, then the low trees, and finally the tallest trees — timed in perfect harmony.

We, too, need to be governed by harmony — harmony with ourselves, with others, and with God. Health, happiness, and spirituality are interrelated. Let us seek to live in the harmony that God offers us all.

Agree with God, and be at peace; thereby good will come to you. (Job 22:21)

Prince of Peace, how can I be at peace with myself, others, You?

Do it today

Procrastination and depression often go hand in hand.

When we're depressed we often feel that we haven't accomplished enough. We feel overwhelmed by all we want to do. We can't decide what to do first — so we do nothing. That makes us *more* depressed and we have even less energy.

To break this vicious cycle, psychologists tell us, we have to act, do something. For example, put away one item in a cluttered room.

Once we take the first step, we feel less hopeless and our energy level begins to rise.

For clinical depression, get medical help. For a simple case of the blues, get going.

I am in distress; my eye is wasted from grief, my soul and my body also. For my life is spent with sorrow. (Psalm 31:9-10,14)

When depression descends, O God my helper, come to my aid.

Everybody reads, everybody wins

"Children who are read to regularly become good readers, and everyone who's ever broken the poverty cycle had a caring adult to help them," says Arthur Tannenbaum.

This retired New York executive organized "Project Everybody Wins" to tutor children with reading problems. In the project, corporate volunteers have lunch with individual pupils once or twice a week and read books to them.

Besides helping youngsters learn to read, the tutoring gives them emotional support. It makes them feel recognized and important.

For children from homes where no English is spoken or from broken homes, it's a real godsend.

Tutoring is just one of many ways volunteers can help change lives.

We know that You are a teacher. (John 3:2)

Remind us, Master, that we are all teachers by the way we live our lives.

Talking without listening

Talking without listening can cause problems.

A couple driving to Maryland made what began as a routine stop in West Virginia. Then the man got back in the van and drove off without realizing his wife was still standing in the parking lot.

The wife enlisted the help of police, who finally spotted the van in Maryland and stopped it. The police asked the man if he had noticed that his wife was missing. He hadn't. He said, "I've been talking to her the whole way and wondered why she didn't answer."

This is an extreme case, but people are often more interested in what they have to say than in listening to other people's ideas.

Get in the habit of listening. It's important to communication and to relationships.

Give ear, O My people, to My teaching; incline your ears to the words of My mouth. (Psalm 78:1)

Open my ears to the gentle whisper of Your voice, Redeemer.

Two good neighbors

Today I want to introduce you to two people who live three thousand miles apart. They don't know each other, but they have something wonderful in common.

Barbara Williams is a security guard at P.S. 94 in the Bronx. For 16 years she has taken the trouble to greet parents and students, encouraging them to be on time, to talk about school and family problems. She offers understanding and practical help, like information on jobs or babysitting. In a neighborhood that knows poverty, drugs and violence, Barbara Williams gives comfort.

Bill Ogburn is a milkman who has delivered good cheer to his customers in Los Angeles for over forty years. He brings groceries to older folks who find it hard to get out. He even offers credit to those who have trouble paying their bill. He says of his customers, "I have a lot of great folks."

Bill Ogburn and Barbara Williams are experts at loving their neighbors.

> **Jesus answered . . . 'You shall love your neighbor as yourself.' (Mark 12:29,31)**

> *Man of Nazareth, help me fulfill the second great commandment.*

Found: ancient wine bottle

Archaeologists recently found some new evidence that drinking wine is a very old custom.

The remains of a large ceramic jar unearthed in the Zagros Mountains of Iran were found to date back to about 3500 B.C. Scientists analyzed some stains on the jar and found that it had been used to store wine. That means wine has been making people's meals festive for well over 5,000 years.

But what adds to festivity when it's used in moderation can bring despair when it's used in excess — and becomes addictive. There's nothing joyful about alcoholism.

If you know someone who's addicted to alcohol, urge that person to get help.

Who has woe? Who has sorrow? Who has strife? Who has complaining? Who has wounds without cause? Who has redness of eyes? Those who linger late over wine. (Proverbs 23:29-30)

Help me use alcohol in moderation, Jesus.

World's best "how-to" book

Now and then I look at a clever ad for some useless item and think, "What a waste of talent!"

It was a pleasure the other day to see an imaginative ad used to promote a very worthwhile product — a special Bible for students.

The ad pictured the Bible, and above it, a cartoon showing a frightened boy on a surfboard, trying to keep his balance on a huge wave.

The caption read, "It doesn't stop life's pounding waves. It teaches you to ride."

The ad went on to say, "Growing up isn't easy. There's a sea of questions . . . Thankfully, the God who loves you has a better solution than getting knocked down and pulled out with the undertow."

This ad reminds us that the Bible is a wonderful "How-To" book on living. Study it.

> **The law of the Lord is perfect, reviving the soul; the decrees of the Lord are sure, making wise the simple; the precepts of the Lord are right. (Psalm 19:7-8)**

Holy Spirit, alert me to the Bible's wisdom.

Children of tomorrow

Anthropologist Melvin Konner offers insight into an adult's view of "Childhood":

"It seems as if we could start taking our uniqueness more seriously . . . We might as well realize that we were not built to feel quite comfortable with ourselves while children are visibly suffering around us.

"Children are living messages we send into the future, a future that we will not see. We understand enough about them now to have a fairly good idea of what they need.

"In fact we are building the house of tomorrow day by day, not out of bricks or steel, but out of the stuff of children's bodies, hearts and minds."

It's true, you know, children are the future. We have an obligation to do our best for them — to assure them healthy bodies and minds and spirits. It's also our gift to tomorrow and to ourselves.

(Jesus said) 'Let the children come to Me, do not hinder them; for to such belongs the kingdom of God.' (Mark 10:14)

Enable us to lead our children to You, Lord and Lover of souls.

Kindness close to home

Did you know that the word "kindness" comes from an Old English word for kin or family?

It's within the home that we first learn to care for one another. Yet it's often those closest to us that it's easiest to take for granted. Marilyn Fanning, writing in Guideposts, tells her family's story. When their youngest son married, Marilyn and her husband Bill invited the couple to live with them while they finished school. Then, Mrs. Fanning's mother broke her arm, so her parents came to stay.

The crowded four-generation household became selfish and argumentative. Finally, Marilyn got everyone together and told them, "We all love one another. We're just not showing much consideration for one another." So, they set some rules and life improved.

Encouraging respect means changing attitude and behavior.

> **We know love by this, that He laid down His life for us — and we ought to lay down our lives for one another . . . Little children, let us love . . . in truth and action.**
> **(1 John 3:16,18)**

Holy Spirit, encourage us to respect each other — even the most difficult among us.

The right scent

Piped-in music is now used in many workplaces to increase productivity. Piped-in fragrances may soon be used, too.

A few years ago, researchers at the University of Cincinnati found that people smelling the piped-in scent of peppermint did better work than those who didn't receive it. A researcher at Catholic University found that peppermint actually stimulates electrical activity in the brain.

But more important than any physical stimulant is the motivation that comes from realizing we can each make a difference in the world.

> **You are the salt of the earth; but if the salt has lost its taste, how can its saltiness be restored? . . . You are the light of the world. A city built on a hill cannot be hid. (Matthew 5:13,14)**

> *Help me, Jesus, add savor to the world by the salt of my life.*

Volunteer to build up

For many college students, spring break is a time for fun in the sun. But some students from Syracuse University decided to spend their time doing something good for people in need.

Twelve members from the University's chapter of Students Offering Service (SOS) went to Massachusetts to work with Habitat for Humanity. That's an ecumenical Christian organization which builds homes that are sold to poor men and women at low cost. SOS members made a difference in the lives of others — and felt the satisfaction it brings.

You can help others by volunteering your time and skills. Check out your area's nursing homes, day care centers, hospitals, or schools. Or find out about long and short-term commitments to organizations like Habitat.

For others, for yourself, do it.

If I then, your Lord and Teacher, have washed your feet, you also ought to wash one another's feet. For I have given you an example, that you also should do as I have done to you. (John 13:14-15)

How may we imitate Your loving service, Jesus?

Delightful, imperfect creation

A group of history buffs recently dedicated a plaque to two stray dogs that died 130 years ago.

These two dogs, named Lazareth and Bummer, were such devoted friends that they captured the hearts of San Francisco citizens. When Bummer died, Mark Twain wrote his obituary, saying that Bummer died "full of years and honor and disease and fleas."

The humorist's wry observation about the canine condition reminds us of the human condition as well. Even the most beloved and saintly among us have our weaknesses.

That's something we forget when we condemn ourselves for falling short of perfection.

God doesn't condemn us for our imperfections, but loves and delights in us.

Who can detect their errors? Clear me from hidden faults. Keep back Your servant also from the insolent . . . Then I shall be blameless. (Psalm 19:12-13)

Loving Redeemer, save me from myself, my pride, my determination to "go it alone" without You.

Integrity at an early age

Sixto Perez is a 12-year-old boy from California who lives in poverty. He often eats only one small meal a day and wears worn-out hand-me-downs. Although he is poor, he refused to take money from a drug dealer who wanted Sixto to work for him.

Sixto lives with his mother and five brothers and sisters in a trailer. He tries to help out his family by sweeping and stocking a grocery store for $20 a week. One day while he was sweeping outside the store, a drug dealer offered Sixto $100 to sell drugs at his school. The boy refused. He told the drug pusher, "I only make a little bit of money, but I do it honestly."

Sixto Perez is a youngster with integrity. Though he was tempted by easy money, he remembered what he had learned about drugs from his family and teachers. His courage offers a good example for adults and children alike.

God will fully satisfy every need of yours according to His riches in glory in Christ Jesus. (Philippians 4:19)

God, fill my every need with the one thing which alone can satisfy them — Your very self.

"This grace of love"

Cardinal John Henry Newman wrote, "My God, the Paraclete, if I differ at all from the world, it is because You have chosen me . . . and have lit up the love of God in my heart. If I differ from your saints, it is because I do not ask earnestly enough for your grace, and for enough of it, and because I do not diligently improve what You have given me. Increase in me this grace of love . . ."

You know, we could each make the same observations. But as Cardinal Newman knew, there is a solution.

We can find the oil of grace for our lamps if like Cardinal Newman we pray and pray and pray — with gratitude for what we have, with a joyful anticipation of the time given to prayer, ceaselessly and confidently.

Our good God always gives to those who ask.

> **(Jesus) told them a parable, to the effect that they ought always to pray and not lose heart. (Luke 18:1)**

> *Inspire me to pray ceaselessly and with confidence, Holy Spirit.*

Attracting attention

You probably won't be surprised to learn that the huge stereos some teenagers have in their cars can be deafening.

These "boom boxes on wheels" typically have a sound level of around 120 decibels. That's far above the level known to damage the hearing.

Why do teenagers want such loud stereos in their cars?

"To attract attention — anybody's attention," one teenage boy admitted frankly.

Young people have a special need for recognition. If it isn't forthcoming, they try to get attention any way they can.

Give the young people in your life recognition and encouragement for any and all positive contributions.

> **May the God of steadfastness and encouragement grant you to live in harmony with one another. (Romans 15:5)**

> *What makes for disharmony in my relationships with those closest to me, Holy Spirit? Help me to know and work to resolve problems.*

Mission on wheels

When we see a biker on a motorcycle, many of us think of negative stereotypes like outlaw gangs. But if you're riding the roads near Arlington, Texas, you may meet a motorcyclist with a mission.

The Full Gospel Motorcycle Association International consists of 600 motorcycle riders from all over the world who are dedicated to increasing religious faith and helping stranded motorists. Members help drivers by providing food or water, a jump start, or a ride to get gas. They often leave behind a religious pamphlet or a message that simply says, "God Loves You."

How often have we judged someone by their looks, their friends, or by their ethnic background? Take the time to really get to know someone. It can enrich your life.

> **Do not judge, and you will not be judged; do not condemn, and you will not be condemned. Forgive, and you will be forgiven; give, and it will be given to you.**
> **(Luke 6:37-38)**

> *When it is difficult not to judge, not to condemn, and when forgiveness is even more difficult, God, help me!*

Reaching out — long distance

It is possible to nurture long distance friend-ships and family ties.

Phone regularly, even if it's only to listen.

Write, include news items, recipes, photos, any-thing the person would like to receive.

Remember special days with a small gift or a card.

Keep a list of preferences to help you select cards and gifts.

Congratulate family and friends on their achievements.

Support them by means of your communica-tion when they're having difficulties.

Plan to visit if possible and let distant family and friends know well in advance. Anticipation is sweet. And welcome their visits, too.

It's worth the work to maintain long distance relationships. God does!

I bow my knees before the Father, from whom every family in heaven and on earth takes its name. (Ephesians 3:14-15)

Heavenly Father, bless parents with respect for their children; children with respect for their parents and each other.

Butterflies and raindrops

People may find rainy weather depressing, but for a butterfly, a rainy day is a *real* downer. It can't fly in rain. It just has to take cover and wait out the rainstorm.

Big raindrops and heavy wind can injure its delicate body. And it needs sunlight to function.

If its body temperature is less than 86 degrees Fahrenheit, it can't fly. When the air is cooler than 86 degrees, it has to warm up its flight muscles. Ideally, it does this by sunning itself. If there's no sunlight, it has to waste precious energy shivering its wings.

Just as butterflies need the sun, people need the warmth of God's love. Hope is the confidence in God that lets us *feel* His love even when clouds hide it from view.

I will not forget you. See, I have inscribed you on the palms of My hands. (Isaiah 49:15-16)

God, I need Your warm embrace now.

Nothing trifling about truffles

Father Pierre Gleize is delighted when parishioners drop fungus into the collection plate. His parish is in southern France, and the fungus given as an offering is truffles. This gourmet delicacy commands such a high price that it's called "black diamond." The parish's offering of truffles is sold to raise funds.

In a homily, Father Gleize told churchgoers in this truffle-producing area, "Christians should embellish the world the way truffles embellish a meal. Love transforms everything. Isn't that just what a good truffle does to an omelette, pate or poultry dish?"

One person's goodwill *can* add a special joy to the lives of others. Love is truly the ingredient that transforms everything.

> **Jesus answered him, 'Those who love Me will keep My word, and My Father will love them, and We will come to them and make Our home with them.' (John 14:23)**

> *Redeemer, may our love for You find its expression in loving service.*

Using gifts and opportunities

Tony Pena, the respected catcher for the Boston Red Sox, is a native of the Dominican Republic who learned all about baseball from his mother.

She made sure all her children finished their schoolwork and chores every day. She then would teach them the rudiments of baseball in a nearby field.

One day the family lost their land because of a failed crop. Tony Pena prayed to God and asked Him to give him a chance to help his family. When the Pittsburgh Pirates offered him a spot on their farm team, he went to America. He was homesick — but his mother sent him letters with words of encouragement and advice on baseball.

Tony Pena realized that God had given him the chance that he asked for, so he made good use of his opportunities. Use yours to make this world a better place.

**God, the Lord, is my strength.
(Habakkuk 3:19)**

Infuse me with Your strength, Lord of Hosts.

Ways to make yourself sick

Do you want to be sickly? Then hug anger, resentment, fear, worry, guilt, and jealousy tight.

Be sure to be self-preoccupied. Cultivate feelings of inferiority and of not being loved.

Avoid creative activities.

Do all you can to dominate everyone, everywhere, all the time.

But if you want to be healthy in mind, soul and body — let go of anger, resentment and jealousy.

Forget yourself in the service of others. Learn to value yourself as the Child of God you are. Know that you are loved, by God and others.

Cultivate whatever creativity you have — it is God's gift to be used to the glory of His name.

And, as the saying goes, "live and let live." There's no need or reason to dominate anyone, anywhere. God's in charge! He orders everything to your good.

> **There is none like God ... who rides through the heavens to your help ... He drove out the enemy before you.**
> **(Deuteronomy 33:26,27)**

> *God the Lord, is indeed my help. I will not fear.*

Bad ad — good catch

Carl Safina was disturbed by an ad for outboard motors. In the ad a fishing guide was saying he ran his motor in flats — shallow water.

Safina wrote the company explaining that no experienced fisherman would run a motor in flats, damaging these areas where game fish feed. He said the ad made the company look irresponsible.

As a result of Safina's letter, a new ad was substituted, one that encouraged respect for the marine environment.

A letter from one concerned reader changed a large corporation's advertising strategy. Is there a letter you've been meaning to write? Send along your praise, constructive criticism or thanks. It can make a world of difference.

If you continue in My word . . . you will know the truth, and the truth will make you free. (John 8:31-32)

O You who made Leviathan and all the other beings of the sea, enable us to appreciate how connected we all are.

Concerts without walls

An unusual Dutch orchestra called the Ricciotti Ensemble toured in America one summer.

It plays not in concert halls but in the street, and in places such as parks, hospitals, prisons, and centers for the homeless. Audiences include travellers, drug addicts, handicapped persons, seriously ill children.

The 40-piece orchestra is made up of music students, professionals, and amateurs of all ages. Since it was founded in 1970, the group has been bringing beautiful music to people who might otherwise have no chance to attend concerts.

We all have special gifts of some kind that we can share with others. Discover and enjoy them.

As in one body . . . all the members do not have the same function, so we . . . having gifts that differ according to the grace given to us, let us use them. (Romans 12:4,6)

Come Holy Spirit, show us what our gifts are and enable us to use them for God's glory.

A happy meeting

To be memorable, events must be recalled and retold. And one hopes that 3-year-old Alexandra's recent trip to New York City's theater district will indeed be memorable.

She and her Mother had come from a distant part of the city to buy theater tickets as a 75th birthday present for Alexandra's grandfather.

As she was sitting in her stroller, a majestically tall creature with taut muscles approached. His hooves clopped gently on the asphalt. The mounted police officer relaxed his grip on the reins and a long graceful neck stretched toward Alexandra. She was startled. Then the softness of the horse's nose and the gentle feel of his rubbery lips on her knees entranced her. Sterling, the police horse, was just curious — and friendly.

It's not every day a city child is gently nuzzled by a horse. Hopefully, Alexandra will remember the occasion happily.

A child who gathers in summer is prudent. (Proverbs 10:5)

In the summer of their lives, enable children to gather delightful memories, Child Jesus.

How to cheer your spouse

Here are some suggestions for pleasing your spouse — and yourself.

● Create your own special holiday, maybe the anniversary of your first date.

● Become your spouse's cheerleader when he/she has had a horrible day.

● Tell your spouse, "I love you," and really mean it.

● Sit on the same side of a restaurant booth.

● Share an intimate conversation away from the family chaos.

● Do something your spouse thinks you've forgotten.

● Drop everything and do something for the one you love — right now!

Whatever you do, do something special for your spouse and you'll be doing something special for your marriage and your mutual happiness.

I am my beloved's and my beloved is mine. (Song of Solomon 6:3)

Loving Lord, You have given spouses to each other as best of friends, loving companions on life's journey. Help them to cherish and nourish that friendship.

"Stand and Deliver" — education

Many of you may recognize the name Jaime Escalante from the hit movie, "Stand and Deliver." Edward James Olmos starred in the biographical film about Escalante, a math teacher who taught advanced-placement calculus to kids who had been labeled as hopeless and unteachable.

Escalante received national attention for his unorthodox but effective teaching methods. He uses visual aids, mental games, and after school study sessions to make sure his students are learning. He also gets parents involved by calling them at home — sometimes as early as 5 a.m. — when a student is truant or lazy.

Jaime Escalante is a successful teacher because he believes his students can learn, regardless of the obstacles before them. He is living proof that parents and educators can work together to encourage students to do their best.

Your word is a lamp to my feet and a light to my path. (Psalm 119:105)

Word of the Father, light my path so that I may always walk in love.

Salute to fair play

It's encouraging to hear about athletes who consider fair play more important than winning.

For instance, the British kayak team lost the world championship race in 1990. The thing that caused them to lose the race won them the Pierre de Coubertin International Fair Play Trophy.

The British team was in second place in the race, with the Danish team leading. Then the Danish team's rudder was damaged and the British team stopped to help them fix it.

The race continued, and the Danes beat the British by one second! If the British had taken advantage of the other team's accident, they would have won. But they valued fair play more.

The *real* winners, in sports and in life, are those who show nobility of spirit.

So run that you may obtain (the prize). (1 Corinthians 9:24)

Courteous Lord, give me a share of Your courteousness even as You give me the ability to run the race and receive the prize — life eternal.

Kids and creativity

What would you do if you had named 700 kids, had 200 more to name and had run out of ideas? As an added challenge most of your kids were female, so you'd need feminine names.

Recently Susan Cahn faced just this challenge. She'd used "sensible" names like Mary Ann and "frivolous" ones like Peony. But there were still 200 unnamed kids and an American Dairy Goat Association requirement that all goats registered with it have a name.

So one Saturday Ms. Cahn brought some of the kids to a New York City farmers market figuring that shoppers would have fresh ideas for kids' names.

We don't know how many kids were named but it was a creative solution to a vexing problem.

Look for a creative solution to your problem.

The Lord God formed every animal of the field and every bird of the air, and brought them to the man to see what he would call them. (Genesis 2:19)

With Your help, Lord God, no solution to a problem is impossible. Enlighten and strengthen me.

Illustrating the face of pain

Portraitist Lin Baum brings her canvases, oils, easel and self to the world's war zones and slums. Her subjects?: children of want and war, children with a name and history, eager to be recognized as the human persons they are. Despite everything, they are Baum's patient models and fascinated observers.

Baum says, ". . . until we start valuing each other as people, everything is just gonna go to hell . . . our salvation is to rediscover our own humanity."

She continues, "it is only when we can think about suffering in terms of someone with a name and a unique identity that we can gain a sense of solidarity with those in need."

Baum puts her words into action by using her artistic skills and talent. But each of us can do the same with our unique skills and talents.

Suffering *does* have a human face.

Rejoice insofar as you are sharing Christ's sufferings. (1 Peter 4:13)

If I can not yet rejoice to share Your suffering, Jesus, at least enable me to carry them with patience.

A wholesome way to age

It is possible to cope with inevitable aging in a wholesome, positive way:

- Stop criticizing yourself; it's limiting.
- Associate with those who make you feel good.
- Smile, especially when you don't want to.
- Learn something new as often as possible.
- Volunteer for at least a few hours a month.
- Read a book a month and visit the library regularly.
- Work; be involved.
- Eat a prudent diet.
- Exercise as health (and budget) permit.
- Be sure to consume enough water and juices; they're good for the skin and prevent dehydration.

Aging is a natural process with which you can cope; and which you can even enjoy.

The righteous flourish like the palm tree . . . They are planted in the house of the Lord; (and) . . . in old age they still produce fruit. (Psalm 92:12,13,14)

My heart, sink your roots deep into the Lord, that you may flourish even in old age and sickness.

Meet a new role model

Most retail stores have ads and catalogs featuring attractive models wearing fashionable clothes. But some models in ads for Nordstrom, Eddie Bauer, and Target have something extra — wheelchairs.

These stores and others began featuring models with disabilities around 1990. Since the Americans with Disabilities Act became effective, disabled models have become even more visible. There are 34.2 million physically challenged American consumers and until recently, they were rarely seen in ads.

Besides attracting disabled consumers, ads like these provide role models for the disabled, says Shannon Bloedel. She is a disabled skier who has modeled for Nordstrom and Eddie Bauer.

What can you do to provide accessibility and acceptance for a disabled person?

I put on righteousness . . . I was eyes to the blind, and feet to the lame. (Job 29:14,15)

Merciful Savior, how can I provide accessibility and acceptance for even one disabled person?

A giant junk food addict

A junk-food addict recently crashed a gradua-
tion party. When he shambled into their camp-
ground, campers literally showered him with
cookies and candy bars.

His appetite whetted, he crashed another gradu-
ation party albeit four days late and sat surrounded by the trash sacks. "He would eat out of one,
then another, like a little smorgasbord," said a
state wildlife officer.

But finally the bear with the sweet tooth was
lured by marshmallows and shot with a tranquil-
izer. He was released later in a more rural and
candy-free area.

As a reporter said: "Makers of junk food are
missing out on a very big market: black bears"!

What are we so very fond of — bearish about
— that it could be called an addiction and put
us in harm's way?

> **Do not desire the ruler's delicacies, for they
> are deceptive food . . . be wise enough to
> desist. (Proverbs 23:3,4)**

Divine Liberator, free us of our addictions.

Guilty conscience, then honesty

Octavio Sandoval is a 17-year-old who was among the many people who looted during the Los Angeles riots.

Octavio stole three beds from a furniture store so he and his younger siblings would have a place to sleep. He felt that stealing the beds would mean doing something for his family.

But a guilty conscience and disapproval from his parents made him return the mattresses to a local church four days later. Octavio's story ran in the L.A. Times. As a result, many people who were moved by Octavio's situation called in to offer financial support and beds for his family.

Stealing and violence cannot be excused. But we can learn to understand why people do what they do in order to survive. Try to understand, and to help out where you can.

Do not repay evil for evil or abuse for abuse. (1 Peter 3:9)

Help us, Jesus, to understand people's motives.

Good day's start

One morning recently, the conductor on a Manhattan-bound subway train announced the station, then continued in a cheerful voice, "A good morning to you all. And this is a good morning."

He went on to give astonished passengers a detailed weather report and a morning news update, including a sports report — all with a lively touch of humor!

His good humor seemed contagious. Passengers' sour expressions began giving way to smiles. The conductor helped a trainful of people start their day in a good mood.

Use your sense of humor to lighten the load of others.

Rejoice in the Lord always; again I will say, Rejoice. Let your gentleness be known to everyone. (Philippians 4:4-5)

Jesus, fill us with joy and gladness.

Creating personal peace

To achieve inner peace . . .
- don't idolize your difficulty
- accept your helplessness
- admit only you can change yourself
- stop fruitless thinking and talking
- look to others for support
. . . and most importantly,
- do what you can.

No difficulty is insurmountable. But you do need a positive attitude. Patience helps, too.

And remember the most important "other" who will support you if you only ask — He's too courteous to force His help on you — is God.

As Teresa of Avila once said, "who has God, lacks nothing" — including the ability to achieve peace.

> **You who live in the shelter of the Most High, who abide in the shadow of the Almighty, will say to the Lord, 'My refuge and my fortress; my God, in whom I trust.'**
> **(Psalm 91:1-2)**

> *Sheltering God, I do trust in Your care; strengthen my trust.*

A step ahead of death

In May of 1991, a group of Holocaust survivors broke their decades of silence. They are called "The Hidden Children," Jewish youngsters given by their parents to the care of others, often strangers, in order to save them.

At their gathering in Manhattan, they spoke about their experiences, trying to help each other understand.

Dr. Magna Denes is now a successful psychoanalyst, but at the age of ten, she was hidden by the Red Cross and other compassionate people in Nazi-occupied Budapest.

"All hidden children consider their survival a miracle," she says. Dr. Denes felt throughout her wartime fears and adventures that she was always one step ahead of death.

The men and women who lived through pain and tragedy and were denied a normal childhood bear witness today to the power of courage, endurance and love.

I know their works and their thoughts, and I am coming to gather all nations. (Isaiah 66:18)

Gather the afflicted into the shelter of Your everlasting arms, Most Holy One.

Alliance of mutual support

The problems faced by mentally ill people and their families are often complex and frightening.

As a result of their difficulties, the National Alliance for the Mentally Ill was formed in 1979. One goal of the organization is to provide peer support for families of the mentally ill as they face day to day questions as well as society's stereotypes. Their other aim is to serve as a voice in influencing government policy as it relates both to issues concerning those who are mentally ill and the demands of public safety.

Today, the National Alliance for the Mentally Ill has a thousand chapters with more than 130,000 members. If you or a loved one needs support, reach out.

There are others who can understand and help.

Do justice . . . love kindness. (Micah 6:7)

Enable those who are mentally ill and their families and loved ones to reach out for help, Lord who inspires many to justice and kindness.

Cheers for super students

If it seems like every other day we hear more bad news about American education and the quality of today's students, here's a change of pace.

In California there's an annual ritual called the Academic Decathlon. High schools compete against each other in a variety of subjects through a series of competitions. One portion, "The Super Quiz," is open to the public and generates as much enthusiasm, noise and even cheerleading as a major athletic event.

The young competitors' preparation is no less rigorous than sports: they take special classes and field trips and study together as often as six days a week.

The coach of the Palisades High School team said: "It's important to the kids to work hard. Plus it's nice to look good in public."

It is nice for anyone to have hard work and achievement noticed.

Those who devise good meet loyalty and faithfulness. (And) in all toil there is profit. (Proverbs 14:22-23)

Help us, Holy Spirit, to reward hard work and achievement.

What must be done

Dr. William Perl has done many things in his 84 years. He has been a psychologist, an attorney, a soldier and a public servant. But his most remarkable achievement occurred when, from 1937 to 1944, Dr. Perl spearheaded an operation which saved an estimated 40,000 Jews from the hands of the Nazis.

While based in Vienna, he arranged for sailboats, freighters, even cattleboats to transport Jews from Europe to Palestine. Though he risked his life time and again, Dr. Perl does not see himself as a hero.

His philosophy is no-nonsense, yet capable of achieving the impossible: "If a situation appears hopeless do not think what can be done. Do what must be done."

Sometimes the only way to make it through hard times is by turning hopelessness on its head.

I appointed you a prophet to the nations. (Jeremiah 1:5)

Lord, make us attentive to the prophets You send among us.

Rich beginnings

In his book "You Don't Have to Be in Who's Who to Know What's What," humorist Sam Levenson said this about his childhood:

"Speaking for myself, and perhaps for some other alumni of the slums, I must declare that I was not a poor child; I just didn't have any money."

He goes on to describe a family who were loving and supportive, who had high ideals and cared deeply about others.

A recent study confirms that what is most important to a child's future success and happiness is not economic status, but warm, loving parents.

Each child deserves such riches. Endow every child in your life with the treasure of your love. It's the legacy of a lifetime.

Let us not love in word or speech but in deed and truth. (1 John 3:18)

Loving Lord, enable parents to love their children generously, sincerely and impartially.

Wanted: a laugh

Let's laugh! Here are some classified ads that will get you started chuckling:

"SNAKE FOR SALE — eats anything and is fond of children.

"WANTED — Man to take care of cow that does not smoke or drink.

"3-YEAR-OLD teacher needed for pre-school. Experience preferred.

"WANTED: Hair-cutter. Excellent growth potential.

"STOCK UP AND SAVE. Limit: one.

"USED CARS: Why go elsewhere to be cheated? Come here first!

"DINNER SPECIAL — Turkey $2.35; Chicken or Beef $2.25; Children $2.00."

Humor — it's the spice of life, the leaven of a day lived well.

> The ransomed of the Lord shall return . . . singing; everlasting joy shall be upon their heads; they shall obtain joy and gladness. (Isaiah 51:11)

Put a smile on my lips, a merry twinkle in my eyes, a song in my heart, Father most holy.

From grief to action

It's not just circumstances that shape our lives. How we react to those circumstances is even more important.

Ann Salerno of New Jersey had the misfortune of losing her mother, who died of cancer when Ann was 13.

Instead of simply being overwhelmed by grief, Ann was motivated to do something positive. She decided she was going to study medicine, so she could help save lives. But it would be many years before medical school. So, believing her mother's death was linked to environmental pollution, she became active in her school's recycling program — and works to raise community awareness about environmental protection.

She channeled her grief into helping others.

(The Lord) did not despise or abhor the affliction of the afflicted; He did not hide His Face from me, but heard me when I cried to Him. (Psalm 22:24)

Thank You, Lord, for caring for me as though I were the only person in the world.

Old time market and atmosphere

The nursery rhyme begins, "To market, to market . . ." That's where people used to meet each other, discuss events, and shop.

That's still true for the 8,000 residents of Hastings-on-Hudson, New York. The Hastings Prime Meats shop "reminds some of a general store, where anonymous company or a familiar face can always be found."

Elbow-to-elbow customers find that conviviality comes easily. Graciousness is valued over speed without slighting the customers. And the owners are always around.

Its secret? Hastings Prime Meats is small, human-scaled, a mom-and-pop type place that invites sociability.

Strive to create the atmosphere in which sociability can thrive in your life and work. The world will be a better place for your effort — and so will you.

Agree with one another, live in peace . . . Greet one another with a holy kiss. (2 Corinthians 13:11-12)

What can I do, Carpenter of Nazareth, to be a better neighbor?

Constructive change for volunteer

Miguel Santiago was spray-painting graffiti on a subway train when he saw a poster describing New York's City Volunteer Corps for young people. He put down his spray can and read the poster.

Now he's busy with City Volunteer Corps projects like renovating parks, helping the elderly, and tutoring children in day-care centers.

It's hard work, but it's giving him a good feeling to earn respect and gratitude from others — and gain a feeling of purpose and self-confidence.

There are lots of youngsters like Miguel — full of energy and creativity, but in need of a little guidance about how to use it constructively.

Helping young people channel their energy in a constructive direction can change their lives — and the world — for the better.

> **(Jesus) took a little child . . . in His arms, (and) He said to them, 'Whoever welcomes one such child in My Name welcomes Me, and whoever welcomes Me welcomes not Me but the One who sent Me.' (Mark 9:36-37)**

> *Child of Nazareth, how are we to welcome You in the children we meet?*

Beauty found in flaws

Do you tend to measure yourself against others and think of your differences as imperfections?

Next time you're belittling yourself, remember what gives emeralds their beautiful color: a trace of an "extra" element that also makes them flawed.

Emeralds are a form of the common mineral beryl. What makes emeralds different is that they contain a small amount of chromium. The chromium atoms replace some of the aluminum atoms found in beryl crystals. Since the chromium atoms are larger, they squeeze the crystal structure, cracking it. But they also give the emerald its distinctive color and make it a valuable gem.

The small traits that make us "different" also give us our individuality — our special qualities that can add beauty to the world.

Fear Not, O Jacob My servant, says the Lord, nor be dismayed, O Israel; for lo, I will save you . . . and you shall be My people, and I will be your God. (Jeremiah 30:10,22)

Creator who delights in diversity, help me delight in my own uniqueness and that of my fellow human beings.

Learning — at a circus

For 19 years, a theater troupe from San Francisco called Make-A-Circus has made audiences laugh and learn. The circus performers act out plays filled with acrobatics and clowning. Then they conduct workshops for the audience in juggling, stilt walking, and acrobatics.

This year, the theme of the show is literacy. The plays center around characters who have to fight off a villain who wants kids to waste their time on video games and TV instead of reading. Peggy Ford, the artistic director of Make-A-Circus, said, "We thought what was important to get across was that knowledge is freedom."

She's right. Knowledge gives you the power to do almost anything you put your mind to. And knowledge doesn't end when you finish school. Discover a subject that interests you and start learning about it today.

Take my instruction instead of silver, and knowledge rather than choice gold; for . . . all that you may desire cannot compare with (wisdom). (Proverbs 8:10-11)

Guide my learning, Wisdom of the Father.

Words from home

People around the world associate New York's Times Square with New Year's Eve festivities and Broadway's bright lights. Many thousands of visitors and residents of the city know it is also home to Hotaling's News Agency.

It's a one-of-a-kind store that stocks hundreds of newspapers and periodicals from across North America and dozens of foreign countries.

The current owner, Arthur Hotaling, says his grandfather started the business in 1905. He had decided that a city made up of folks from everywhere might want to read their hometown papers. He was right.

There is always something special about home and about those close to us who make up our family. But it's also true that they can be the easiest people to take for granted. Today, tell them you love them.

They who have My commandments and keep them . . . will be loved by My Father, and I will love them and reveal Myself to them. (John 14:21)

May my loving observance of Your commandments give evidence of my love for You, Jesus.

Portrait of a busy woman

We are told that until recently women married, raised families, kept house, were good wives, and never developed personal careers.

But Sofonisba Anguissola, a 16th century Italian noblewoman, was among those who prove that it is possible to do everything expected of women and have a flourishing career.

One of six sisters to be given a boy's education in the arts, music and letters, Anguissola was then apprenticed to an artist. There followed study with the great Michelangelo; appointment as a court painter; marriage and a large family.

And in her 90's she was not only still painting but teaching others, among them Van Dyck.

Over 400 years ago Sofonisba Anguissola found that marriage, family and career can be compatible.

Whatever decisions you make about how to live your life, give it your all.

> **Strength and dignity are her clothing . . . She opens her mouth in wisdom . . . She looks well to the ways of her household, and does not eat the bread of idleness.**
> **(Proverbs 31:25,26,27)**

> *Jesus, son of Mary, bless women who combine family, marriage and career responsibilities.*

Mobile care for moms

"Project Mothercare" is an unusual clinic on wheels that operates out of a 48-foot tractor-trailer. This van provides free medical care to pregnant women in poor sections of New Haven, Connecticut — a town with the highest infant mortality rate in the nation.

The success of the van has been encouraging to St. Raphael's Hospital, which operates it. Of the babies born to mothers receiving care at the van last year, not one died or required intensive care at a hospital.

This van offers pregnant women examinations and treatment, counseling, and help in obtaining aid. It doesn't offer or advise women to have abortions. The purpose of Project Mothercare is to save lives.

Do what you can to support and celebrate life.

(Jesus) went about all Galilee, teaching . . . preaching the gospel of the kingdom and healing every disease and every infirmity. (Matthew 4:23)

Heal us of all our infirmities of spirit, mind and body, Divine Physician.

Sounds of success

People often equate fame with success. But not John Coltrane. This famous jazz musician of the 60's and 70's said: "My goal is to live the truly religious life and express it in my music. My music is the spiritual expression of what I am — my faith, my knowledge, my being."

Coltrane loved jazz because it's a music that changes and develops in the playing. He said, "There are always new sounds to imagine, new feelings to get at. And always there is the need to keep purifying these feelings and sounds . . . so we can give to those who listen . . . the best of what we are."

That's the essence of real success, not only in jazz but in life — developing and giving to the world our very best.

> **As Moses lifted up the serpent in the wilderness, so must the Son of man be lifted up, that whoever believes in Him may have eternal life. (John 3:14-15)**

> *God, enable me to imitate Your generous love.*

ABC's of courage

You may know Curtis Aikens as the green grocer on ABC-TV's *Home* show. What you may not know is that he overcame illiteracy.

Aikens graduated from school but lost many jobs because he couldn't read. He eventually enrolled in ABC's PLUS literacy program. He learned how to read and that led to jobs at a Georgia newspaper and then at an Atlanta TV station.

One day while co-hosting the *Home* show, Aikens was reading from a teleprompter and stumbled over a word. He became flustered and broke down during the live broadcast. Later, he explained what had happened. Hundreds of phone calls came in — all with words of encouragement and support.

Illiteracy is a problem that affects over 27 million American adults. If there is a literacy program in your area, extend your help.

Tell us, how did you write all these words? (Jeremiah 36:17)

What can we do, Jesus, to help illiterate people read and write?

Discovering magic in paper

When Lillian Oppenheimer's daughter was recovering from meningitis back in 1930, her mother looked for a way to entertain her. She found it in origami.

Mrs. Oppenheimer's interest in the Oriental art of paper-folding continued over the years. By the 1950's, her hobby had gained her publicity, and the popularity of creating beautiful pieces of art from sheets of paper had spread across America.

Today it is even used in therapy classes where it offers a sense of accomplishment and satisfaction. From simple to complex, the forms range from fantasy dragons to birds in flight to geodesic balls.

Mrs. Oppenheimer borrowed an art form from another culture, and finding magic in a piece of paper, invited others to enjoy her hobby.

Beauty is part of life. Seek it out to enjoy and share.

Ah, you are beautiful, my love.
(Song of Solomon 1:15)

Yes, God, You *are beautiful — You are beauty itself.*

Perspectives on writing

When you have to put something in writing, if you worry about the impression you're making, you're not alone. Many people feel self-conscious about their use of language.

Writer John Luther offers a few suggestions for making your words on paper sound like you: "For easy reading, keep your sentences short. Use contractions the same as you do when you're talking. Say things before you write them. Then read them aloud after they're written."

"What distinguishes great writers is not their vocabulary or scholarly phraseology," says the author. "What makes them outstanding is what they have to say and the clarity and interest with which they say it."

Our words can have a great affect on others, whether written or spoken. And each and every word is worth handling with care as they leave us to reach another.

The fruit of the Spirit is love, joy, peace, patience, kindness, goodness, faithfulness, gentleness, self-control. (Galatians 5:22)

Holy Spirit, enrich me with Your gifts.

Along the trail

This year, the Sierra Club celebrates its 100th anniversary. The club was founded as an effort to protect and conserve national areas in the environment.

Several members of the club are celebrating its centennial by hiking the entire length of the Appalachian Trail. The scenic trail is 2,100 miles long and cuts through 14 states from Georgia to Maine. It has altitudes of over 6,000 feet.

The goal of these hikers is to get more people involved in environmental protection. "I don't think you can get people interested in protecting the environment unless you get them to appreciate it," says Harvard Ayers, a Sierra Club member.

God has given us many beautiful areas — learn to appreciate them and do what you can to protect them.

As you did it not to one of the least of these, you did it not to Me. (Matthew 25:45)

Master, give me the grace necessary to be a wise steward of what You've given me.

Night out for unemployed

You've heard of special promotional events at baseball games, such as "Cap Night." The San Diego Padres tried a new fan appreciation event when they held "Unemployment Night."

The local unemployed were treated to a free baseball game and also got free hot dogs, drinks, and sandwiches. The promotion was sponsored in order to lift the spirits of the jobless people in the area who don't have extra money to spend on entertainment. About 2,500 unemployed people showed up at the stadium.

Though it didn't provide any jobs, this free baseball game did cheer up many downhearted people. If you have a friend who is jobless, why don't you help him or her out by offering your encouragement and company? Have them over for dinner, treat them to a movie or take a walk together. They'll appreciate it.

Let love be genuine . . . love one another with mutual affection. (Romans 12:9,10)

May I extend Your own encouragement and companionship to an unemployed neighbor, Jesus.

Grounding graffiti

The high school in Bayside, New York, used to be covered with graffiti — the walls, even the ball courts. Then students got tired of having their school look bad and organized a group called "Operation Graffiti Storm."

These volunteers, aged 10 to 17, paint marked-up areas and try to convince other young people that graffiti is not art but vandalism.

Four young graffiti offenders are now doing community service under the group's supervision. One of these reformed vandals says the project has helped him turn his life around.

As soon as new graffiti appears, Operation Graffiti Storm members attack it with paint. They say they'll fight until the battle is won.

Positive action is making a real difference.

If anyone among you wanders from the truth and is brought back by another, you should know that whoever brings back a sinner . . . will save the sinner's soul from death. (James 5:19-20)

Lord, make me a means of Your reconciliation.

Delight found in dandelions

In May each year, a town in West Virginia holds a dandelion festival to celebrate spring.

Dandelions seem an appropriate symbol of spring. They appeal to the spontaneous, joyful side of our nature. They begin life drifting freely in the wind. They sail over orderly rows of hedges and settle on monotonous green lawns — brightening them with random patches of yellow flowers.

While many gardeners do not welcome them, other folks find them truly attractive. Why?

For most of us, tight schedules and daily routines are essential. But we need to pause now and then just to enjoy the beauty of the present. Moments spent sharing laughter or relaxing in the sun or listening to music brighten our day. The joy of such moments lifts our hearts in spontaneous praise to our Creator.

> **No one is worse than one who is grudging to himself . . . My child treat yourself well according to your means . . . Do not deprive yourself of a day's enjoyment.**
> **(Sirach 14:6,11,14)**

Thank You, God, for the beauty of each moment!

Cohousing for cohesion

A group of families in Colorado are trying a plan called "cohousing." It combines the support of group living with the privacy of separate housing.

Homes are clustered around a central courtyard or park. Residents share chores like babysitting and home repair. And they take turns preparing the evening meal, which is eaten in a common dining room.

But group living has drawbacks as well as advantages. The Colorado families learned this early, when they disagreed about a color scheme.

In any kind of group undertaking, there are likely to be conflicts that grow out of differences of one kind or another. But when people attack the problems instead of each other, they're on the way to solving them.

Maintain constant love for one another, for love covers a multitude of sins. (1 Peter 4:8)

When love becomes difficult, Redeemer, may we continue to love because You first loved us.

Models for the brain

The PET scan is a device that shows which parts of the brain work hardest during a task. It's revealing a lot about the way we learn.

Studies confirm that basic learning patterns are formed early in life. Between the ages of two and ten, according to Michael Phelps, one of the PET scan's developers.

For instance, people think in the languages they learn at an early age. Languages learned later have to be translated by the brain.

Behavior patterns are also formed early in life. As Phelps points out, that may make undesirable behavior hard to change later.

We're realizing more and more how important parents and teachers are — not just in imparting knowledge, but in serving as good role-models.

If I speak in the tongues of mortals and of angels, but do not have love, I am a noisy gong or a clanging cymbal.
(1 Corinthians 13:1)

Father, make it possible for parents, teachers, all adults to be good role models for children and teens.

Stick out your neck

It's not always easy to speak up, to do what needs to be done. It can mean exposing ourselves to criticism, even abuse. People willing to take the risk deserve encouragement and help.

The purpose of The Giraffe Project is to give them encouragement. This group publicizes the efforts of "giraffes," people who stick their necks out for the common good. The publicity is meant to help the projects of these people — and to inspire others to follow their example.

Two men in Virginia are among the "giraffes" publicized. The men saw lots of potatoes going to waste and decided to do something about it. Through their efforts, over 15 million pounds of surplus potatoes have been distributed to the needy.

Be a "giraffe." Help change the world.

My Father is glorified . . . (when) you bear much fruit. (John 15:8)

Jesus, enable us to be fruitful vines in the Father's vineyard.

"If I were you . . ."

The founder of the world-famous Mayo Clinic, Dr. Charles Mayo, made a valuable rule for himself. "When I am your doctor," he said, "I try to imagine the kind of doctor I'd like if I were you. Then I try to be that kind of doctor."

That's a good idea, whoever we are or whatever we do. It's easy to forget that we don't all think the same way or have exactly the same feelings about problems — or even about good things. There's a big difference between asking yourself "How would I feel in that situation?" and "How is that person feeling and how would I want to be treated if I felt that way?"

Staying sensitive to the needs of others sometimes demands a lot of us. But a kind and generous spirit is worth cultivating.

> **Love is patient and kind; love is not jealous or boastful; it is not arrogant or rude. Love does not insist on its own way.**
> **(1 Corinthians 13:4-5)**

Make me a genuine lover, Loving Lord.

Finding real happiness

Most people would probably agree that they want to be happy. But defining what happiness is, what it means to us and how to grasp it, isn't easy at all.

Here are a couple of ideas that might stir your own thinking. "It is an illusion to think that more comfort means happiness," according to writer Storm Jameson. "Happiness comes of the capacity to feel deeply, to enjoy simply, to think freely, to risk life, to be needed."

And the author of many American classics, Nathaniel Hawthorne, believed that "happiness is a butterfly, which, when pursued, is always just beyond your grasp; but which, if you sit down quietly, may alight upon you."

However we describe it, happiness comes to us not by seeking it, but by living lives of loving action.

Happy are those . . . (whose) delight is in the law of the Lord, and on His law they meditate day and night. (Psalm 1:1-2)

That You and Your law might indeed be my delight, Lord, my joy.

Going beyond the limits

Andrea Friedman is a young woman with Down's Syndrome who overcame the odds that were set against her.

When she was born, some doctors recommended that she be placed in an institution. Her parents decided against it. They placed her in a regular school, took her to the opera and the ballet, provided her with acting lessons, and painstakingly taught her how to drive.

By the time she was 21, Andrea was studying child psychology in college and had a recurring role on the TV series "Life Goes On."

We all have limitations in one way or another, and sometimes we let these obstacles get in the way of achievement. If we have faith and believe in ourselves and others, we can all accomplish far more than we might have dreamed.

Do not be anxious about your life, what you shall eat, nor about your body, what you shall put on. For life is more than food, and the body more than clothing . . . Fear not, little flock, for it is your Father's good pleasure to give you the kingdom.
(Luke 12:22-23,32)

How can I realize more fully just for today the Father's care for me, Lord Jesus?

Learning the language of nature

A flower is not just a flower according to naturalist Forbes Watson. He defined the color, shape, smell and tactile sensations of a flower as its "sensuous" nature.

But he also said that each flower is a living being with its unique way of surviving; of growing, from seed, bulb or tuber; of spreading by climbing, clumping, rambling, or standing solitary; even of wilting and dying.

Watson called these the "symbolic language," and the "hidden nature" of a flower which whispers of something beyond the individual flower we see.

It's the same with people. We see their appearance, hear their speech, observe their manners. But do we see beyond to their unique, hidden nature: how they survive, grow, age and even die?

Cherish your own uniqueness and that of every created being.

Why do you pass judgment on your brother or sister? Or you, why do you despise your brother or sister? For we will all stand before the judgment seat of God. (Romans 14:10)

May the unique beauty of each flower remind me of the unique beauty of each human being, Creator.

Giving others hope

In 1973, Betty DellaCorte-Ryan was a woman who seemed to have it all. Two lovely daughters, a fine home — and an alcoholic husband who abused her.

Even though she had left him before, she had always returned. And the abuse continued. Finally, through the support of Al-Anon, the national support group for relatives of alcoholics, she was able to help herself and others.

She opened the first treatment center designed just for victims of domestic violence. In the years since then she has started organizations to shelter women and youngsters, care for children from troubled homes, and counsel abusers.

One woman found the courage to help herself and her children through the support of others. She's returned that gift of a new life to many others.

Deal courageously and may the Lord be with the upright! (2 Chronicles 19:11)

Jesus, courage, please.

Our street, our responsibility

There was so much trash and broken glass along Springfield Street in Lawrence, Massachusetts, that Steven Clarke was afraid that his two young sons would cut their feet.

So he joined with two elderly neighbors and spent a long day filling barrels with debris and sweeping the sidewalks and streets. Both older men have health problems, but persisted in their task. One said, "Maybe people will think twice about throwing something down."

While nobody thought one cleanup would solve the problem permanently, neighbors were happy with the results and the efforts of the three volunteers.

Steven Clarke said all he wanted was a safe place for his children to play. "It's my block. It's my street," he said. That's a good reason for any of us.

Whoever knows what is right to do and fails to do it, for him it is sin. (James 4:17)

How can I express my concern for my neighborhood, God?

On stage — and on the line

Seven years ago, Sharon Brisnehan left her job as an electronics technician in a factory. She wanted to use her creativity, so she decided to try her hand at stand-up comedy.

But even as she worked on her comedy routines over the next few years, she began to notice more and more street people in her city of Denver. She commented to her daughter, "This is getting out of hand. Something's got to be done." Her daughter asked, "Why don't we volunteer at the Samaritan House?" Soon they were active at the shelter. Then they brought Mrs. Brisnehan's mother and grandmother along as well. Now four generations are involved in helping homeless people.

Sharon Brisnehan believes that on the stage "you put yourself on the line and at the shelter you do also."

Think about putting yourself on the line for your beliefs.

For a little while you may have to suffer . . . so that the genuineness of your faith . . . may redound to praise and glory. (1 Peter 1:6-7)

In times of trial and testing, Mighty Lord, keep my faith in Your person and message strong.

Fishing — or fishy — story

A California businessman caters to people who want to catch fish, but don't have the patience for fishing.

He provides a pond, fishing poles, and fish. There's no waiting to catch a fish. And it requires no skill or effort. A customer chooses a fish and it's fastened on a pole. All the customer has to do is pull the fish out of the water.

A serious fisherman who doesn't think this can be called fishing says, "That's like filling a pheasant full of lead balls so it can't fly, then stepping on it, and saying, 'I got a pheasant.' "

To call pulling in fish "fishing" is something like defining success as bringing in money. Real success is more than that. It's developing our skills and talents and using them well.

(The) book of the law shall not depart out of your mouth; you shall meditate on it day and night, so that you may be . . . prosperous, and . . . successful. (Joshua 1:8)

May my loving adherence to Your will, Lord, be the basis of my success and prosperity.

Spread the word: someone cares

A while back, New York's Hunter College decided to encourage the students who were staying up late to study for exams by serving a midnight breakfast. The college's president at the time thought it was such a good idea she helped dish out bacon and eggs to the hungry students.

Some people asked if it would undermine authority to be seen in that role. The president replied, "It makes us seem real. I think knowing someone cares that you do well on your exams is the message I should get across."

"Someone cares" is an important message and a powerful motivator. Knowing that one person takes an interest in another's welfare can be an incentive.

And each of us is capable of being that caring person for somebody else. Kindness does count.

He who closes his ear to the cry of the poor will himself cry out and not be heard. (Proverbs 21:13)

May we understand that kindness to someone who is needful — of our time, our talents, our love, our sympathy, even our treasure — is kindness to You, Merciful Savior.

Happily ever after

Why do people cry at movies with happy endings? Psychologists say it's not because these people feel happy, but because they feel sad.

According to psychologists, a happy ending reminds us of the idealized picture of the world we had as children. We once believed everything could be perfect in our lives. And we feel sad that life hasn't turned out that way.

In this world people never just "live happily ever after." Expecting to is a sure way to make ourselves unhappy. When we measure our lives against the yardstick of perfection, they are bound to fall short.

Problems and disappointments are a part of life. But they need not make us unhappy if we accept them as a way we learn and grow.

The Lord disciplines those whom He loves, and chastises every child whom He accepts . . . He disciplines us for our good, in order that we may share His holiness. (Hebrews 12:6,10)

That I might learn from life's difficulties to rely on God and not on myself, Holy Spirit.

Up and over obstacles

To most of us, not having a right hand would make playing baseball seem impossible. But not to Jim Abbott, New York Yankee pitching ace and star of the 1988 gold-medal-winning U.S. Olympic team.

He never felt that being born without a right hand made him different from other kids. He wanted to play baseball, and he didn't let his handicap stop him from trying. He says, "You can't be worried about failing, because failure is a part of life. You just have to keep trying."

Abbott advises others, "Never think of anything as impossible until you've worn out every single possibility . . . An obstacle is simply a step you have to climb over to achieve your goal."

This is good advice. Fear of failure can be our greatest handicap.

I sought the Lord, and He answered me, and delivered me from all my fears. Look to Him and be radiant. (Psalm 34:4-5)

Yes, Lord, deliver me from all my fears.

Young people "doing some good"

The activities of Chi Phi fraternity at Lehigh University include more than having fun. The group is doing something constructive — literally.

Its members are working with the Hellertown, Pennsylvania, Historical Society to restore a Colonial-era gristmill.

The students enjoy the change of pace and the chance to work with older people. And, as one participant commented, "You get to realize you're accomplishing something."

The fraternity's president is proud of their work. He said, "It shows we are capable of doing some good, and not just having parties."

Volunteer work of many kinds can give us the satisfaction of knowing that we're making a positive contribution to the good of others.

Do what is good. (Romans 13:3)

Lord, how can I "do what is good" in my present circumstances?

Developing our inner lives

According to pollster George Gallup we have six spiritual needs:

● to believe that life is meaningful and has a purpose

● to have a sense of community and deeper relationships

● to be appreciated and respected

● to be listened to — to be heard

● to have practical help in developing an adult faith

● to sense that one is growing in faith

Are these your spiritual needs? . . . Or the needs of those you know? And if they are, what are you doing to satisfy these legitimate spiritual wants? To pray is to begin to fulfill all your requirements, spiritual and otherwise.

(Be) rich toward God. (Luke 12:21)

Jesus, enable me to so order my life that I satisfy my spiritual needs first.

When not to speak

Silence. It is defined as the total absence of speech. But Native Americans could teach us another: the *selective* absence of speech.

Apaches, among others, kept silent when meeting strangers, in the company of the recently bereaved, in the initial stages of courtship, among relatives and friends after a long separation.

Such silence is the language of listening to the other with one's entire being.

They also kept silent in response to shouted insults and criticism.

This silence says much about peace and self-control.

The world could be a better place if each of us practiced this kind of silence. Selective absence of speech is a language of respect and love.

(There is) a time to keep silence, and a time to speak. (Ecclesiastes 3:7)

Enable me to appreciate the selective absence of speech, Word of the Father.

"Know yourself"

Jesus said that "the truth will make you free." An inscription on the temple of Apollo at Delphi, Greece, read "Know yourself." The philosopher Socrates said that the "unexamined life is not worth living."

And Lao Tzu, the founder of Taoism, explained:

"It is wisdom to know others;

"It is enlightenment to know one's self.

"The conqueror of men is powerful;

"The master of himself is strong.

"It is wealth to be content;

"It is willful to force one's way on others.

"Endurance is to keep one's place;

"Long life is to die and not perish."

Self-knowledge shows us ourselves as we really are. It can teach us both humility and self-esteem. Have you grown in self-knowledge today?

The truth will make you free. (John 8:32)

Come, Holy Spirit, come teach me to know myself and so to grow in humility and self-esteem.

Teacher speaks volumes

Elementary school teacher Lucia Rede Madrid believes that "all children deserve books." Since the impoverished town of Redford, Texas, had no library, Mrs. Madrid started one herself.

The town's largely Mexican-American population struggled to survive on tiny farms, and Mrs. Madrid wanted a better future for their children.

Despite her efforts, a library had never been set up, so after she quit teaching, she decided to start one in her husband's store. The library began with 25 books of her own. Through her efforts, it grew to over 15,000 volumes, replacing canned food on the store shelves.

In 1990, Mrs. Madrid received two Presidential medals for her work. She brought the town more than just a library. She brought it hope.

'Will you not receive instruction and listen to My words?' says the Lord. (Jeremiah 35:13)

Holy Spirit, what can we do to satisfy children's natural hunger for knowledge?

An ancient blessing

About forty-years-ago a shepherd discovered the library of a first century Jewish group that had lived in the Judean desert near Qumran. Among these Dead Sea Scrolls, as we now know them, is an expansion of the so-called priestly blessing in the sixth chapter of Numbers.

It reads, "May the Eternal (God) bless you with every good and keep you from all harm. And enlighten your heart with discretion in life. And be gracious unto you with everlasting knowledge. And lift up a kindly countenance towards you for eternal peace."

Could there be any better way to celebrate a friend or family member's birthday than by praying this blessing for them? Goodness, discretion, knowledge, eternal peace *are* the best gifts we could want to share.

> **The Lord bless you and keep you . . . make His face to shine upon you, and be gracious to you: The Lord lift up His countenance upon you, and give you peace.**
> **(Numbers 6:24-26)**

Bless us, Lord our God.

"Use me as an example"

Gail Devers won the gold medal for the USA in the 100-meter race at the Olympics in Barcelona. This came just a year after her feet came close to being amputated.

Ms. Devers became ill in 1988. She was misdiagnosed as having fatigue. A doctor finally recognized that she had Graves' disease, and began radiation treatments for a large cyst on her thyroid.

She resumed training in 1991 but her feet, which were burned and swollen from the radiation, were so bad that they started shedding skin. The problem was so severe that if she had waited any longer for treatment, she would have needed amputation. She had to stay completely off her feet for three months.

When she returned in time for the Olympics, she ran her personal best and won the gold. Gail Devers said, "Use me as an example. If you have faith and never give up your dream or goal, anything is possible."

**With God all things are possible.
(Matthew 19:26)**

God, help me to experience that indeed with You "all things are possible."

Profile of a "typical" American

When you hear polls and statistics that talk about the "typical American" do you ever wonder just who that is? Well, the New York Times compiled census bureau data, opinion polls and marketing surveys to come up with one profile.

Since over 51 percent of the population is female, we are looking at the Average Jane. She is 32.7 years old, married and a mother. She is a high school graduate who is a clerical worker for a private company.

She lives in the suburbs in a mortgaged house with two televisions. Last week she watched over 28 hours of television, but did not attend church services, though she does belong to a church.

While few people would match this profile exactly, many of us could see a bit of ourselves here. That makes it all the more amazing and wonderful that we each remain unique individuals.

God created humankind in His image, in the image of God He created them; male and female He created them. (Genesis 1:27)

Thank You, Creator, for making me the unique person that I am.

Guide to contented living

The famed German writer Goethe offered a list of nine requisites for contented living. They are as timely now as they were when he wrote them 200 years ago.

"Health enough to make work a pleasure. Wealth enough to support your needs. Strength enough to battle with difficulties and overcome them.

"Grace enough to confess your sins and forsake them. Patience enough to toil until some good is accomplished. Charity enough to see some good in your neighbor.

"Love enough to move you to be useful to others. Faith enough to make real the things of God. Hope enough to remove all anxious fears concerning the future."

Goethe showed wisdom in these thoughts, perhaps especially in the use of the word "enough." Often we seek something more, when contentment could come with gratitude for having enough.

There is great gain in godliness with contentment; for we brought nothing into the world, and we cannot take anything out of the world. (1 Timothy 6:6-7)

Grace me with contentment, Jesus, for after all I do have everything in You.

Work for a worthwhile world

Don Henley is a talented singer and songwriter and a concerned environmentalist. He is the founder of the Walden Woods Project, a movement devoted to saving the land made famous by writer Henry David Thoreau.

The Massachusetts area is being threatened by overdevelopment. Henley's efforts to preserve the land include several concerts, a book, and a 10-kilometer walk. Each has raised money and awareness about the situation.

We can all protect our environment by doing simple things, like recycling and carpooling.

Learn about more ways and pass them along to your family and friends. The more everyone knows about how we can save the earth, the more we can make a difference.

The heavens are the Lord's heavens, but the earth He has given to human beings. (Psalm 115:16)

Creator, show us how to be wise caretakers of the earth.

Together in God's love

Compassion is a virtue which seems to be lacking in our country today. Sadly, judgmentalism and self-righteousness have taken over and claim new victims daily.

Some believe that those with AIDS deserve their suffering, that God is punishing them.

But when you think about it, you have to agree with the Rev. Ann Williams, a Southern Baptist chaplain at New York City's Lenox Hill Hospital who says that Jesus "loves these people to pieces. We're all God's children, and the differences do not condemn us."

She also says that nothing can separate us from God's love — "No matter what we do, that love is just there."

Jesus advised only those without sin to cast the first stone. For the rest of us, He advised love.

'Let him who is without sin . . . be the first to throw a stone at her.' (John 8:7)

Lord, let us remember that mercy is one of Your qualities and should be one of ours, if we are to call ourselves Your children.

Thou shalt take care of thyself

Here are some new commandments for good health, courtesy of cardiologist Stephen Yarnall.

● Thou shalt exercise thy body. Walking is free, practical, fun and requires no equipment.

● Thou shalt exercise thy mind. Read. Write. Reflect. Create. Exchange ideas with others.

● Thou shalt exercise thy spirit. Read the Scriptures. Be a lover. Give. Receive. Balance solitude, sharing and group activities.

● Thou shalt play. Find time for fun every day. Have days exclusively for recreation.

● Thou shalt not fear the future. "For (God) will command His angels . . . to guard you in all your ways." (Psalm 91:11)

● Thou shalt not fear the past. "You have cast all my sins behind Your back." (Isaiah 38:17)

Life is for living and loving; for praying and playing. To do so is to thank the Giver!

Always and for everything (give) thanks in the name of our Lord Jesus Christ to God the Father. (Ephesians 5:20)

For life, for love, for the need to pray, for opportunities to play — thank You, Creator.

On compulsive eating and walking

An unusual kind of compulsive overeating recently came to light. Some people eat in their sleep.

At a sleep disorders center in New York City, a few people were found to be sleepwalkers with a special destination. They walk to the *kitchen* and eat large amounts of food — without ever waking. Most of these people are on special diets. They stick to the diets while they're awake, but can't control their desire for food when they're asleep.

Compulsive eating doesn't usually take such a strange form, but it's an addiction that can cause health problems. Many compulsive overeaters have found help in the twelve-step method that has proved successful for alcohol and drug abusers, in groups such as Overeaters Anonymous.

If you suffer from any addiction, seek help.

'Daughter, your faith has made you well; go in peace and be healed of your disease.' (Mark 5:34)

Divine Physician, cure us of our addictions.

Problem behind the anger

The things people seem to be angry about are not always the things really bothering them.

An 11-year-old boy screamed at his mother that she ought to get a better job, that he was tired of being poor. Since they were *not* poor, his mother knew that wasn't the real problem.

Then she noticed the broken light on his bike, and that his bike helmet was too big and wouldn't stay on. For months the busy single mother had put off taking care of these things. A talk with her son confirmed that it *was* things like these making him feel deprived. She immediately took steps to remedy them.

For good relationships, it's important that we try to understand the reasons behind anger — other people's and our own.

Let everyone be quick to listen, slow to speak, slow to anger, for your anger does not produce God's righteousness. (James 1:19-20)

Enable us to understand the reasons for our anger, Holy Spirit.

Rich brew of diversity

Loggers in the Pacific Northwest now prefer espresso to plain coffee. Lines of pickup trucks wait at drive-through espresso booths in Cascade Mountain towns.

This strong, steam-brewed Italian coffee was once rarely found outside cosmopolitan areas. Its growing popularity in remote mountain towns reflects the special flavor of American life.

Ours is a nation of people from many different lands. And they have brought with them the foods and beverages of those nations. Their foods have enriched the American cuisine just as their varied heritages have enriched American culture.

Get to know recent immigrants in your community and make them feel welcome. The diversity of our people makes our country special.

> **You shall not wrong a stranger . . . for you were strangers in the land of Egypt. (Exodus 22:21)**

> *How can we be more genuinely welcoming to strangers, Lord of the Exodus?*

A wave and a welcome

If you are ever in Laguna, California, be sure to look for a friendly fellow who says hello to all the passersby. He is the unofficial "greeter" of the seaside resort town.

He goes by the unusual name of No. 1 Unnamed Archer, which is on his birth certificate because he was an unexpected twin. For more than a decade, he has stood on the corner for 14 hours a day, 7 days a week, waving to pedestrians and motorists. Laguna has a history of greeters dating back to the 1880's.

Mr. Archer meets and greets folks out of love for people and the community. And that love is felt by all who receive his greeting. As one recent visitor told the L.A. Times, "Just the gesture of saying hello makes you feel good."

Is there a new member of your church? Or a new family in your neighborhood? Become a "greeter" yourself. Do what you can in your church or community to make new people feel welcome.

Greet one another with a kiss of love. (1 Peter 5:14)

May we greet one another with the kiss of love expressed in kindliness and good deeds, Jesus.

Leading a humane life

Values, ideals, standards, are the stuff of a truly humane life. The most crucial are:

● a love of *truth* leading to a just, inclusive and progressive world . . .

● a sense of *justice* which recognizes the rights and needs of all . . .

● a spirit of *cooperation* founded on goodwill and right human relationships . . .

● a sense of *personal responsibility* for civic matters . . .

● a dedication to *the common good* recognizing that what is good for all is good for each . . .

True, these values can be defined to include everyone or to exclude all but a favored few. The challenge is to live a definition of these values which includes others through generosity and goodwill.

Walk in the way of the good, and keep to the paths of the just. For the upright will abide in the land, and the innocent will remain in it. (Proverbs 2:20-21)

Lord, lead me in "the way of the good", "the paths of the just."

Home-style supper time

Friends, let's face it, the family dinner is an endangered species — if we allow the TV, lack of time, bickering children and famished adults to kill it.

But according to Dr. Susan Friedland, a child psychiatrist, "Eating together . . . imparts a sense of belonging." And, she continues, "with our busy lifestyles, it may be more necessary than ever for children to feel that there is order, that parents are running the show."

Here are some suggestions for family dinners: make it "supper" eaten in the kitchen; keep the menu simple and appealing to all; have other food available for the picky eaters, and be flexible about the length of supper time.

Family togetherness is important. Build it.

Happy is everyone who fears the Lord . . . You shall eat the fruit of the labor of your hands; you shall be happy, and it shall go well with you . . . Your children shall be like olive shoots around your table. (Psalm 128:1,2,3,)

Father, bless all families everywhere.

Wisdom through the ages

Over the years many unusual books have made it to the New York Times best-seller list, but, perhaps, none as surprising as "The Art of Worldly Wisdom: A Pocket Oracle." The author is Spanish Jesuit priest Baltasar Gracian who has been dead more than 300 years.

A language professor who is a great fan of the book attributes its current popularity to its disinterest in both joy and ambition and its rather melancholy tone. All are feelings that many modern readers can identify with.

Among the quotes: "An ounce of prudence is worth a pound of cleverness." And, this timely comment, "In all the world, the greatest services are now the least rewarded."

Figuring out our place in the world and determining our own measure of success concerns people of every age.

> **'Take care! Be on your guard against all kinds of greed; for one's life does not consist in the abundance of possessions.' (Luke 12:15)**

Redeemer, help me know the true measure of my success.

Fathers: nice work

A recent "Hagar the Horrible" cartoon strip has Hagar lamenting, "I don't create anything in my line of work . . . and when I'm gone, what will I leave behind me? Nobody'll ever say, 'That guy did nice work.' "

Then, while his children run to hug him, his wife comments, "You do nice work."

And you know, she's right. Children are as much their father's "nice work" as their mother's. How much time he gives them. How much tenderness. How much love. How much appreciation. How much freedom to be themselves and not his clones. How much respect. And, importantly, how much he teaches them to relate to others and themselves with respect and maturity.

Fathers, when children are born your creativity's just begun.

> **Fathers, do not provoke your children to anger, but bring them up in the discipline and instruction of the Lord. (Ephesians 6:4)**

> *Heavenly Father, show earthly fathers how to "do nice work" with their children.*

Values start at home

We have heard a lot of talk about the lack of "family values" in our society today. USA Today asked some experts about which values are most important in a family.

One professional believes that we have let our careers interfere with our families. Longer working hours have caused us to spend less time with our families.

A Harvard professor thinks that community support is lacking. He believes that we should help our neighbors.

Another person suggested that we often do not accept the diversity of American families, such as single parents, elderly parents, and racially mixed families. He believes that negative reactions to non-traditional families lead to poor judgment.

Think about your own family. Are you spreading ideas of prejudice and indifference — or tolerance and respect? Loving and healthy attitudes that we share in our own families can help us outside the home.

> **There is one lawgiver and judge . . . who then, are you to judge your neighbor? (James 4:12)**

> *Merciful Savior, help me not to judge myself or anyone else but rather leave the judging to You.*

Former homeless person helps hungry

We all know about the plight of the homeless, but one woman in Chicago is trying to help by using her own experience of homelessness.

Cynthia Hosch gets up at 3 a.m. every Thursday and cooks a hot and nutritious assortment of food. She brings the food to the crowds of homeless people who gather to eat and pray with her in a small park. She tries to show them that they can make it with the Lord's help.

Ms. Hosch does this act of kindness because she knows what it's like to be homeless. She became penniless when she lost her job, her husband, and her home. She lived on the streets for a while until she sought help from a church. Through church members she found work that enabled her to get a small apartment. Now she shows her appreciation by using part of her salary to help the homeless in her neighborhood.

Cynthia Hosch is living proof that one person can make a difference.

Support your faith with goodness . . . and mutual affection with love. (2 Peter 1:5,7)

May we support our faith with goodness and love expressed in making our world a better place, Lord.

One droplet at a time

A small village in an arid section of Chile gets its drinking water by catching fog in nets.

Canadian and Chilean researchers have set up 50 huge sheets of plastic mesh in the mountains above the village of Chungungo. This mesh traps tiny droplets of water from fog and channels the water through pipes to tanks below.

The droplets are so small it takes 10 million of them to form one drop of water the size of a matchhead. Yet droplet by droplet, the 50 sheets catch more than 2,000 gallons of water a day.

It's something to remember. We may feel that what we can do to help others doesn't really amount to much. But one little kindness can lead to another and another — until the total result seems almost miraculous.

Faith, hope, and love abide . . . and the greatest of these is love. (1 Corinthians 13:13)

Lord and Lover, may my love imitate Yours.

Life's eternal questions

In October, 1990, Boruch Teldon had a double-lung transplant operation in hopes of curing the cystic fibrosis which was killing him. But complications developed and eight months later he died. Boruch was 13 years, two months old.

His parents, Orthodox Rabbi Tuvia Teldon and Chaya Teldon wrestled with Job's very question: WHY? And as Rabbi Teldon expressed it they concluded, "Each person is given exactly what is needed . . . to accomplish their purpose . . . Boruch was born with cystic fibrosis, and that was part of his purpose.

"Some people require a second to fulfill it. Some require a hundred years. A person who dies young has a purpose to die young."

Each of us was given life to do something no one else can do. What's your unique role in life?

The righteous, though they die early, will be at rest, For . . . understanding is gray hair for anyone. (Wisdom of Solomon 4:7,9)

Oh, that by "understanding" I might give You glory, Lord of Life!

Be your child's booster

Parents, here are some tips for building your child's self-confidence.

● Identify areas in which your child is especially proficient, whether academic or athletic or artistic.

● Reinforce your child's areas of special proficiency.

● Introduce your child to a variety of hobbies, clubs, musical instruments, sports.

● Gently and respectfully help your child improve his or her appearance. Make suggestions about hair and clothes, but respect your child's ideas, too.

● Be physically present for those events in which your child is a participant.

Remember, the Creator has entrusted another person to you to support and cherish.

Encourage the fainthearted, help the weak, be patient with them all.
(1 Thessalonians 5:14)

Encourage parents in their challenging role, Creator.

A dream and a plan

Barbara Lewis had a dream for success and she set out to fulfill it. At the age of 37, desperately poor and without options, she and her four kids packed their bags and moved from a small town in North Carolina to Los Angeles.

When they arrived there, they had to go on welfare. With the help of financial aid, Barbara Lewis enrolled in community college. She survived poverty by studying by candlelight and doing laundry in the bathtub.

Despite the odds against her, she completed her Bachelor's degree at the University of Southern California. After ten years of struggling, the Lewis family is finally off welfare, and through a scholarship, Barbara Lewis is pursuing her doctorate in English.

She spoke at Los Angeles Community College when she received an outstanding alumna award. Her message of hope was simple: "If you dream, you can develop a plan. And with that plan, the dream becomes the truth."

Whom have I in heaven but You? And there is nothing upon earth that I desire besides You . . . God is the strength of my heart and my portion for ever. (Psalm 73:25,26)

Lead me, Lord.

Making a day of rest

Jesus said that the "Sabbath was made for humankind." Our challenge is to own our Sundays.

Begin by greeting Saturday's sunset or fading light and Sunday's dawn, alert to the expectancy of the holy hour. Marvel at Creation. Notice Sunday's sunset.

Try to make Sunday a day at *your* disposal.

Study the Scriptures, especially the Gospels.

Attend church services, perhaps as a family.

Include art — Dante called it "almost God's grandchild" — and music in your Sunday.

Savor choice foods and good company at relaxed meals.

Be joyful. Play.

But mostly, r-e-l-a-x in that present moment which is Sunday.

If you turn back . . . from doing your pleasure on My holy day, and call the Sabbath a delight and the holy day of the Lord honorable . . . then you shall take delight in the Lord. (Isaiah 58:13)

Lord of the Sabbath, how may I, in this time and place, honor Your holy day?

New slant on Golden Rule

Explaining the Golden Rule, a Gospel narrative says that a certain man was going down from Jerusalem to Jericho . . .

Here's a Buddhist prayer worth considering that includes "every living creature" and "all the world" along with that unfortunate traveler as our neighbor.

It reads in part, "Let no one deceive another / Let no one despise another . . . / Let no one, from antipathy or hatred, wish evil to anyone at all. / Just as a mother, with her own life, protects her only (child) from hurt / So within yourself foster a limitless concern for every living creature. / Display a heart of boundless love for all the world / In all its height and depth and broad extent / Love unrestrained, without hate or enmity." The prayer concludes by saying that this is "known as living here life divine."

Today, lift your heart in thought and thanksgiving.

Thanks be to God for His inexpressible gift. (2 Corinthians 9:15)

Yes, God, thank You for the gift of life!

A new way of seeing

Nigel Barley is a scientist who has spent much time among what many would call "primitive" people. In his book called "The Innocent Anthropologist," he talks about his return home.

"A strange alienness grips you, not because anything has changed but because you no longer see things as 'natural' or 'normal.' . . . After months of isolation, polite conversation is extraordinarily hard. Long silences are taken as brooding displeasure while people in the street react quite badly to the sight of a man quite openly talking to himself . . . Seeing oneself suddenly in this light can be a humbling experience."

"A humbling experience" — that's a situation that we can all identify with. Recognizing our humanity can lead us to greater tolerance for ourselves and others.

> **I also am mortal, like everyone else . . . there is for all one entrance into life, and one way out. (Wisdom of Solomon 7:1,6)**

> *That I might rejoice in my humanity, since You valued it enough to take it on for my salvation, Jesus!*

Stretch your way to success

The late world-acclaimed actress Helen Hayes used to tell an intriguing tale about her early days in the theater. A producer told her she could be great — if only she were four inches taller.

So, said Miss Hayes, "teachers pulled and stretched me until I felt I was in a medieval torture chamber. I gained nary an inch — but my posture became military. I became the tallest five-foot woman in the world."

Her new posture gave Helen Hayes a new attitude: "My refusal to be limited enabled me to play Mary of Scotland, one of the tallest queens in history."

It's a good story to remember when facing any limitation. Try to change, to stretch your limits. But if that isn't possible, consider stretching your own attitude.

It could be your key to success.

Do not worry about your life . . . or about your body . . . Is not life more than food, and the body more than clothing? . . . Can any of you by worrying add a single hour to your span of life or add one cubit to your height? (Matthew 6:25,27)

Help me, Creator, accept myself as I am.

Families travel for fun

It seems like summertime is synonymous with family vacations. To make your trip as pleasant and fun as possible, follow these tips from Dorothy Jordon, publisher of the "Family Travel Times" newsletter:

● Look for active vacation places where your kids can make something or use their imaginations.

● Get your children involved in advance by showing them books, guides, or videos of the places you'll be seeing.

● Plan educational activities in the morning and recreational time in the afternoon. Your kids will have more patience after they've had their rest.

● Remember that your kids will learn not only from the places you visit, but from the travel itself.

Vacations should provide fond memories, not nightmares. Plan yours well so your whole family can have a fun time.

There is nothing better for people under the sun than to . . . enjoy themselves, for this will go with them in their toil. (Ecclesiastes 8:15)

Dear Father, help us relax and rediscover the child's ability to play.

Slow down for kindness

A few days after Hurricane Andrew destroyed part of southern Florida, this letter appeared in the Miami Herald from a young woman who had been directing traffic in the city:

"I can't tell you how many thoughtful and generous people are out on the roads. One person after another would slow down to hand me something to drink, water, sodas, ice.

"I also want to thank the man who gave me the traffic whistle. And the man who gave me the handmade orange signal boards.

"People honk and wave and give me so much encouragement. It's just very heartwarming.

"Thanks again from the girl who directs traffic on Dixie (Street)."

The kindness of strangers can make a difference.

Whoever is kind to the poor lends to the Lord. (Proverbs 19:17)

May we remember, Loving Lord, that kindness to strangers is kindness to You who were a stranger and in exile.

Creativity has no age

Charles Bennett is a dramatic example of what older people can do. This 93-year-old dramatist is currently writing a screenplay based on one of his own plays. The earlier version appeared on the London stage more than 60 years ago.

Bennett is fighting the battle against age discrimination in one of its strongholds — Hollywood. He says, "The studio heads think the only people who are really creative are the young."

But he points out that time allows you "to perfect your craft," and that "good ideas aren't exclusive to the young."

Other older people can fight age discrimination as Bennett does. They can refuse to believe that age means loss of ability. And they can *show* that this idea is wrong.

> **Do not cast me off in the time of old age; forsake me not . . . for my enemies speak concerning me. (Psalm 71:9,10)**

> *Ancient of Days, be with Your older daughters and sons, guarding them, cherishing them.*

A little bit better

If you inherited a fortune, what would you do with it? Some people decide to give it away.

New Hampshire teacher Edorah Frazer gave most of her $450,000 inheritance to help those in need. Ms. Frazer was disturbed by the imbalance of wealth and opportunity around her. She said, "I can . . . shift the balance a little bit by my own actions."

When Grace Ross inherited $650,000, she asked community advocates to help her decide how to use it for the good of others. Ms. Ross said, "Whatever is decided, we will come away with good feelings because it's an experience of the human spirit struggling for betterment of the world."

We don't all have fortunes to give away, but we can all give of our time and talents to help make the world a better place.

> **The King will answer them, 'Truly I say to you, as you did it to one of the least of these My brethren, you did it to Me.'**
> **(Matthew 25:40)**

Holy Spirit, guide my efforts to make this world a better place for my being in it.

Thirsting for justice

The late Michael Harrington's book *The Other America* focused attention on the poverty that exists even in a rich nation like ours.

Harrington urged Americans to visualize this nation as it could and should be. He once pointed out that desert peoples can't imagine a society in which water is not scarce and precious. In America, water is plentiful and available to everyone. Nobody dies of thirst.

But, said Harrington, we Americans can't imagine a society in which nobody goes hungry or homeless, a society in which nobody lacks opportunity for a good education or health care.

As Harrington's words remind us, God calls us to visualize and work for such a society. Every citizen can be a voice for economic justice.

Give justice to the weak and the fatherless; maintain the right of the afflicted and the destitute. Rescue . . . them from the hand of the wicked. (Psalm 82:3-4)

Holy Spirit, inspire me to be a voice for economic justice in word and work.

Beauty tip: from the inside

Teenage model Courtney Kennebeck has a valuable beauty tip for people of all ages. In an interview for YOU Magazine, she said:

"Beauty . . . comes from an inner peace. People who are described as beautiful may have nice looks, but if they're not nice people, then you can't really think that they're beautiful. But when they have peace inside and they're happy with themselves, they look more beautiful on the outside."

As this perceptive young model reminds us, beauty involves more than features or figure or fashion. It starts within. Inner peace gives people a radiance that sparkles in their eyes and adds warmth to their smiles.

Inner peace comes when we realize that God loves us, that whatever life brings, we can trust Him.

Fear not, little flock, for it is your Father's good pleasure to give you the kingdom. (Luke 12:32)

Loving Father, enable me to trust You more completely each day.

Revitalizing your time

Here are some ways you can make your life more truly human.

- bring music and laughter into your life
- unlearn cultural sexism, ageism and racism
- learn to communicate openly
- develop your ability to listen
- take time to play, relax, and enjoy nature
- develop your natural talents and interests
- cultivate your unique spirituality
- exercise regularly but moderately
- increase active, creative learning
- eat wisely with an eye to good health *and* enjoyment

It doesn't take much effort to make your life more human. But YOU are worth the effort.

> **What are human beings that You are mindful of them, mortals that You care for them? You have made them a little lower than God. (Psalm 8:4-5)**

> *May the way I live give evidence of my dignity as Your child, God my Father.*

Converting harmful into useful

Hazards can occur in unexpected places.

Old telephone poles are a problem to dispose of because the wood is treated with toxic chemicals like creosote. These can contaminate water.

But now there's a new way to get rid of these poisons. Scientists have developed microorganisms that eat the toxic chemicals in shredded-up poles — converting the poisons to harmless substances. The cleaned wood chips can then be used to make paper.

Negative emotions can also be hazardous. But there's a time-tested way to get rid of the poisonous emotion of resentment. Forgiveness converts resentment into compassion. Forgiveness cleanses us of destructive feelings that can harm us and others.

Forgive, and you will be forgiven. (Luke 6:37)

Jesus, enable me to forgive others. And whom I can not now forgive, do You, Lord, enable me to forgive.

The meaning of words

Cinderella's slippers may have been changed to glass by the sound of a single word.

Scholars point out that only in versions of the story derived from the French does Cinderella wear glass slippers. In other versions of the story around the world, her slippers were made of a more comfortable material: *fur.*

The story was told orally long before it was written. When Charles Perrault wrote down the story in the late 17th century, he probably mistook the old French word *vair,* meaning ermine, for the word *verre,* meaning glass. The pronunciation is the same, though the meaning is different.

A word or two can often make a great difference. Words like "Thank you" and "I'm sorry" can change our relationship with others.

A soft answer turns away wrath, but a harsh word stirs up anger. (Proverbs 15:1)

Make my words gracious, Word of the Father.

Silken thread of hope

In a remote section of Colombia, the war against drugs is being waged with new weapons: silkworms and mulberry trees.

The Cauca Valley has no electricity for industry and no passable roads for getting produce to market. Growing coca (the source of cocaine) gave impoverished small farmers here a way to survive. But it also brought addiction, crime, and violence.

Farmer's advocate Patricia Conway searched for an alternative crop and hit upon silk. She began organizing a project called Silk for Life. They helped farmers bring in silkworm eggs and plant the mulberry trees the worms feed on. Now silk farming is proving successful and is increasing.

By showing farmers a better alternative, one person is helping stop the production of cocaine.

> **There will be . . . glory and honor and peace for every one who does good . . . For God shows no partiality. (Romans 2:9,10,11)**

> *Jesus, enable us to do good, not just for our future glory, honor and peace, but for the good of Your people.*

The secret of good parenting

Eda LeShan is a family counselor, author and longtime friend of The Christophers. For fifty years, she has worked with parents and children, helping them build healthy and happy relationships. So, what is the secret to being a good parent?

Eda LeShan says the key is remembering your own childhood experiences. Look back and learn.

While therapy is needed for serious problems, most parents can benefit from searching their own memories and from asking relatives and lifelong friends what they were like as children.

One mother told the counselor, "After I told my 13-year-old daughter I understood her rebellious feelings and how mixed-up I felt when I was her age, we got along better. But the best part is that I started getting along better with my mother."

Remember the days of old, consider the years of many generations. (Deuteronomy 32:7)

Enable the parents of teens to "look back and learn" from their own teen years, God.

Education to fight AIDS

Jorge and Mariana Serrano are a couple from Puerto Rico who are committed to fighting AIDS. They opened Puerto Rico's first AIDS hospice located outside a hospital.

The Serranos were driven to open the hospice after Jorge, who is HIV-positive, faced housing discrimination because of the disease. The couple has endured harassment, personal attacks and courtroom battles during their six years of AIDS advocacy.

The Serranos have kept up their fight in order to educate people about the disease. Mrs. Serrano said, "Where there is ignorance, there is fear."

If there is one thing we can all learn from AIDS, it is how to be compassionate to each other. Find out the facts about the deadly disease, and how you can help those who have it.

> **I take no delight in your solemn assemblies. . . . your burnt offerings and cereal offerings, I will not accept them . . . But let justice roll down like waters, and righteousness like an ever-flowing stream. (Amos 5:21,22,24)**

> *Divine Physician, enable us to see You in those of our sisters and brothers who have AIDS and AIDS-related complex.*

Save environment — and expense

How can we be better stewards of God's good earth? Here are some suggestions from a United Nations environmental project:

- recycle paper, glass and metals
- reuse egg cartons and paper bags
- avoid disposable plates, cups and utensils
- use rags, not paper towels
- mend and repair rather than discard and replace
- heat your home responsibly
- air-dry your clothes when possible
- use non-toxic, biodegradable soaps and detergents
- buy energy efficient electrical appliances — look for a high EER number

You'll not only be a better steward of creation, you'll save money over the long term.

> 'Who then is the faithful and prudent manager whom his master will put in charge of his slaves?' (Luke 12:42)

Holy Spirit, enlighten my stewardship of the Father's good gifts.

Healing irritations

There's an odd home remedy for mosquito bites. Meat tenderizer that contains papain, an enzyme from papayas, is used to stop the itching.

A zoology professor explained how it works. When a mosquito bites, it injects saliva containing an enzyme that keeps the blood from clotting. Since this enzyme is a protein foreign to the human body, it triggers an immune reaction and the release of histamine. This is what causes the irritation.

When a little meat tenderizer containing papain is mixed with water and put on the bite, it breaks down the foreign protein — and stops the itching.

We often need a remedy for irritations of another kind — those caused by everyday problems and conflicts. The best salve for these is kindness. Kindness has amazing power to soothe and heal.

> **Those who oppress the poor insult their Maker, but those who are kind to the needy honor Him. (Proverbs 14:31))**

> *Dear Maker of us all, let us see Your visage in the needy.*

Successful, no longer shy, guy

When Dave Thomas appears in TV ads for his chain of 4,000 Wendy's restaurants, he doesn't seem like the shy type.

But Thomas has a special sympathy for young people who lack self-confidence. When he was a child, he was so shy he even hid from the mailman who delivered his grandmother's mail. "It's a terrible problem for some kids," he says.

He offers these tips on overcoming shyness:

Don't worry too much about what other people think of you. Take part in group activities. Make friends one at a time. And finally, don't feel shy about praying.

He says, "In our Heavenly Father's eyes we are all equal, and He loves each and every one of us infinitely. God never rejects us."

> **Let each one test his own work, and then his reason to boast will be in himself alone. (Galatians 6:4)**

> *Compassionate Lord, may we be as compassionate toward others as You are toward us.*

In the mood to relax

It seems that even pets can become victims of stress.

In Japan, pet owners can now buy recordings of music designed to soothe their nervous pets. The music is especially composed and performed for this purpose. There's music to relax cats and other music to relax dogs.

Perhaps the nervous pets are reacting to the tension of their owners. We know that children are affected by the mood of their parents, whether it's actually expressed or not. Even we adults respond to the mood of a person we're with.

When we have inner peace, it also spreads outward and touches the lives of those around us. This peace comes from knowing that whatever life may bring, God will be there to help us.

I lift up my eyes to the hills. From whence does my help come? My help comes from the Lord, who made heaven and earth. (Psalm 121:1)

Lord, keep my life from this time forth. I trust in You.

Making life simpler

If you find yourself increasingly overwhelmed by a lifestyle that demands that you own too much, spend too much, rush around too much, you aren't alone.

Father Greg Shuler of Kentucky writes and speaks about the need to simplify and to use material goods for constructive purposes. He suggests that you start with small steps. For example, if your family is too busy to share a dinner together, don't suddenly demand everyone show up every night at supper time. Instead, pick a couple of nights and build from there.

Here are a few other ideas for designing a simpler — and, perhaps, better — life: Stay out of debt, it complicates more than your finances. Buy what you need from companies you consider ethical. If you don't need something, give it away.

And start and end each day in prayer.

Pause and be quiet, My people.
(2 Esdras 2:24)

Teach us to pause a while and rest in You, Jesus.

Having a button on the truth

There's a Jewish tradition that if a person is in doubt about anything, he should just count the number of buttons on the coat or shirt he's wearing. If it has an even number, then he's right. If it has an odd number, he should admit that he's wrong.

There's reason in this apparently nonsensical method. If you have to count buttons to decide who's right, you're going to realize that the conflict doesn't *have* a "right" or "wrong" side. Some conflicts are not about principles but just about differences in taste or viewpoints or needs.

First you have to understand what the real basis of a conflict is. Then you're in a better position to work out a solution.

It is honorable to refrain from strife, but every fool is quick to quarrel. (Proverbs 20:3)

Prince of Peace, make me slow to anger, quick to forgive.

At home — underwater

When Richard Presley is on dry land, some might call him a fish out of water. The 33-year-old Florida man recently broke the world record for living underwater. He spent 69 days in a special pressurized capsule.

Presley was part of a group that was studying the effects of isolation and stress. The others left after 30 days but Presley stayed behind to set the new record.

He even made a few friends in the deep blue sea. One particular fish would peer in the portholes every morning while Presley worked at his computer.

One Navy engineer predicts that we may be living undersea in a few years. There are already underwater hotels for scuba divers.

Scientists like these are helping to shape tomorrow. They are accomplishing things that seemed impossible only a few years ago. If there is something in your life that you've always wanted to do but felt was impossible, reconsider it.

I am continually with You; You do hold my right hand. (Psalm 73:23)

May the knowledge that You, Holy Spirit, are ever with me give me the courage to accomplish the difficult.

Seeing the forests and the trees

As a group of Bronx high school students restore and shape up 60 acres of forest, they're also shaping their lives.

Students working on the restoration project cut down invasive "exotic" vines that are killing native plants. And they build paths and sluices.

Angel Colon, who's had jobs ranging from delivery man to dishwasher, says, "This is the hardest job I've ever had." But he likes being part of a team and feeling that he's accomplishing something important. He says, "Time flies by. Sometimes I feel kind of sad because . . . it's time to go home."

These young people are learning to respect nature; they're learning teamwork and skills; and they're learning to respect themselves.

> **The Lord God took the man and put him in the garden of Eden to till it and keep it. (Genesis 2:15)**

> *You made us stewards of the works of Your hands, Father. Bless our stewardship with genuine wisdom and love.*

Giving with true generosity

When it comes to holidays and special occasions, gift-giving is often an important part of the event. And that has its good points as well as bad.

Dr. Steven Broder, a clinical psychologist in Massachusetts, notes that "Gift giving is a way to reach out and share what we have with others — that's a beautiful impulse that the ritual helps us express. Yet, at some point, that meaning can get lost."

Dr. Broder reminds us that "when you think about the special times in your life, it's not the things you remember; it's experiences with family and friends."

You might decide that it's time to talk it over with your family and friends. Perhaps you'll decide that spending time together in a special way, or giving to those in need makes more sense than buying unnecessary items.

Whatever you do, keep your spirit of generosity.

Love covers a multitude of sins. (1 Peter 4:8)

Holy Spirit, how can I grow in love for others?

Sounds of beauty

On a desolate island off the west coast of Scotland, the sand "sings" when it's touched. Walking across the beach produces a wide range of musical tones, like playing a musical instrument.

Scientists think the structure of the sand creates the sounds. The grains of sand are tiny pieces of quartz, rounded by the sea. Each grain is surrounded by a pocket of air. When the sand is touched, friction between the air and the grains produces musical tones.

We may not have a chance to hear the strange music of singing sand, but we all have a chance to hear the music of rustling leaves.

Happiness need not be pursued in exotic places. The joyful music of God's Creation surrounds us. All we need to do is listen.

The heavens are telling the glory of God; and the firmament proclaims His handiwork. (Psalm 19:1)

Open our ears, Creator, to hear the symphony of Your Creation.

Planting possibilities

In Queens, New York, one July day, a passerby did a double take. Surely that couldn't be an apricot tree in front of that house? But it was an apricot tree, its branches heavy with fruit.

It had an air of unreality here in a city where only the hardiest kinds of trees survive.

Probably no one ever told the homeowners that fragile apricots wouldn't grow in New York City, so they planted the tree — and it flourished.

Many times, the only barrier to our doing something is that we assume it's impossible and never even try. Don't underestimate your ability.

Fear not . . . I will help you, says the Lord; your Redeemer is the Holy One of Israel . . . And you shall rejoice in the Lord; in the Holy One of Israel you shall glory. (Isaiah 41:14,16)

When something seems impossible, Redeemer, remind me that You are with me and can enable me to do the impossible.

Concrete idea paves the way

The town of Bellefontaine, Ohio, literally paved the way for a revolution in transportation.

Thanks to the ideas of George Bartholomew, this little town had the first concrete streets in America — before gasoline driven cars were in use.

Bartholomew came up with a special formula for cement. He persuaded skeptical town officials to let him pave the main streets by donating materials and labor for the first section.

These improved streets, built in the 1890's, opened new possibilities and helped spark the development of the automobile industry.

Important changes often begin with the creativity of one person.

Keep your mind open to new ideas and let your own creativity come through.

Happy is the person who meditates on wisdom and reasons intelligently, who reflects . . . on her ways and ponders her secrets, pursuing her like a hunter and lying in wait on her paths. (Sirach 14:20-22)

Come Holy Spirit, font of wisdom, give us that wisdom which comes from God, Himself.

Because she is needed

We all know of the plight of Somalia, Africa, where many have died and millions more are threatened with starvation. But you may not know of Annalena Tonelli, a woman who has been feeding the hungry and nursing the sick there for nearly 25 years.

Tonelli left her native Italy when she was 25 to live among the poor in Africa simply because there was a need. She is not paid and lives simply with no water or electricity in her clinics. She feeds the malnourished children, treats kids and adults suffering from tuberculosis, and helps poor women weave baskets to sell on the local market. She has stayed all this time even though she has been threatened and robbed during the country's civil unrest.

Annalena Tonelli is one person who is making a difference in this world every day.

Seek justice, correct oppression; defend the fatherless, plead for the widow. (Isaiah 1:17)

How, Just Lord, may I do good and not evil today?

Motorcyclist wants to see it all

Emilio Scotto just finished his first trip around the world and is about to begin his second global journey.

The Argentina native travelled around the world by motorcycle. The trip took 7-and-a-half years and he used 10,000 gallons of gas, changed 59 tires and filled seven passports. He travelled through 142 countries in climates ranging from 130 degrees to minus 29 degrees. He was arrested four times for suspicion of spying and was shot at by snipers. He met Pope John Paul II and Moammar Kadafi. Scotto also married his longtime sweetheart in India.

So with all those memorable experiences under his belt, why is he doing it again? Because he missed 43 countries on his first trip, and he wants to see it all.

Though most of us cannot take such an unusual trip around the world, we can fill our lives with joyful experiences. Try to do something you've always wanted to do, and share the good memories with loved ones.

Rejoice in all the good which the Lord your God has given you. (Deuteronomy 26:11)

Let us rejoice before the Lord our God.

From graffiti to art

Los Angeles has an unusual but successful summer job program. City officials and business owners were trying to combat vandalism caused by teenagers. They went around the city and found kids who were spray-painting graffiti and hired them as artists.

The youths were paid to design socially conscious murals. They analyzed problems and did research for their artwork. Many focused on issues such as education, government, and history. The murals they created are thought-provoking, positive messages. As a result, most of the kids have realized the difference between art and vandalism and the city has gotten some interesting and inspired artwork.

We often hear bad things about today's youth. Rarely are they praised for the good deeds that many of them perform. If there are teenagers in your life or your neighborhood, remember to take notice of the good things they do.

Speak evil of no one . . . be gentle. (Titus 3:2)

How, Jesus, may we speak well of the teens we know?

Creativity is ageless

At age 99, Beatrice Wood received the American Craft Council's gold medal for highest achievement in craftsmanship.

Her ceramics are part of the permanent collections of a dozen major American museums from coast to coast. But perhaps the most interesting thing about her career is that it began at age 40 when she couldn't find a teapot to go with some plates she had bought.

A friend suggested that she take a ceramics class at a local high school so that she could make a matching teapot. And with that simple start, her talent and hard work fashioned a respected reputation for her beautiful designs and crafts.

Age may tell us where we are in life, but never who we are. That comes from within. Today, create as beautiful a day as you can for yourself and those around you.

If one is mean to himself, to whom will he be generous? . . . Do not deprive yourself of a day's enjoyment; do not let your share of desired good pass by you. (Sirach 14:5,14)

Today enable me to "create as beautiful a day" for myself as possible, Creator.

Bowling league of winners

A group of recovering alcoholics meet every Sunday in a Los Angeles bowling alley for fun and support.

The bowling league was formed after one man took up the sport while in rehabilitation. When he was released from the hospital, he realized that there was a need for recovering addicts to get together for good, clean fun. Within a month, 12 teams had signed up.

The bowling league helps many members realize that they can have fun without drinking. One man feels that he is making progress in his recovery because he can see that he can socialize and stay sober. As he said, "This is doing it, not talking about it."

If you have a drinking problem — or another compulsive problem such as overeating, drugs, gambling or spending — there are many support groups across the country that can help. Check your phone book, your local hospital or your church for a group that's right for you.

If you have been raised with Christ, seek the things that are above, where Christ is, seated at the right hand of God. (Colossians 3:1)

Christ Jesus, enable me to find healing.

It takes toughness to teach

Many people are concerned with the shape of education today, so a group of young people is trying to change the schools for the better.

Teach for America is a program founded by Princeton University graduate Wendy Kopp. The program recruits college graduates to teach in the nation's most troubled schools. The young teachers have found out how tough teaching really is. Sometimes they had to buy their own supplies and work with large classes of students, many of whom didn't speak English.

Almost 500 people worked for Teach for America for the first year and 60 percent decided to stay in teaching, even with all the hardships they faced. Some of the others will develop special projects for Teach for America, to try and help schools in other ways.

Many times we take our teachers for granted, without realizing how earnest and dedicated most of them are. Show your appreciation to a teacher you know.

Listen to the voice of (your) teachers. (Proverbs 5:13)

Master, help us learn from all the various teachers You give us.

Mayor who understood people

Fiorello La Guardia was arguably New York's most loved and respected mayor. One reason was his interest and compassion for "the little guy."

Once, when he was presiding over Night Court as he occasionally did, a man was charged with stealing a loaf of bread. The man admitted his guilt, but said he did it to feed his starving family.

Mayor La Guardia told him, "There can be no exceptions to the law. I fine you ten dollars."

Then he reached into his own pocket, adding, "Here's the ten dollars to pay your fine — which I now remit. Furthermore, I'm going to fine everybody in this courtroom fifty cents for living in a city where a man has to steal bread in order to eat."

$47.50 was collected and given to the defendant.

The Mayor understood the power of the individual, and of forgiveness.

Our Father in heaven, hallowed be Your Name . . . forgive us our debts, as we also have forgiven our debtors. (Matthew 6:9,12)

Enable us to be forgiving people, Jesus.

Gardens out of garbage

Where most people see garbage dumps and vacant lots, Cathy Sneed sees gardens of vegetables and flowers. The founder of San Francisco's Garden Project works with former prisoners, drug addicts and gang members to grow and tend gardens in the inner city.

Ms. Sneed works with her streetwise students to help beautify neighborhoods and also to help people. She believes that hard work and watching things grow can help show them that they can be responsible and create something good. She herself was a young single mother, a dropout, and a welfare recipient who eventually worked her way through college. She believes that desiring change and keeping busy are the keys to success. As she puts it, people are successful when they "see that what they do matters."

What each of us does *does* matter — and each one of us has the power to change things for the better. Is there a way you can help someone in your community?

> **If a brother or sister is naked and lacks daily food, and one of you . . . (does) not supply their bodily needs, what is the good of that? (James 2:15-16)**

> *Holy Spirit, how can I put my faith into action?*

Youngsters consider problems of hunger

Here is a statistic that is as appalling as it is overwhelming: in the 1980's one hundred million people died from causes related to hunger.

To encourage school children to consider the plight of starving people, A World Food Day essay contest was begun.

One third grader wrote that "if we all just give a little, it would help the world a lot." Another thought that well-fed men, women and children should remember to "be happy for the food you eat."

A seventh grader believes that "world hunger is a war that is always raging. And just maybe someday this war will be history."

That's a big goal and right now it's a long way off. But that doesn't mean that each day each of us can't make a difference in this fight for life.

> **If a man is righteous . . . gives his bread to the hungry and covers the naked with a garment . . . withholds his hand from iniquity, executes true justice . . . and is careful to observe My ordinances — he is righteous. (Ezekiel 18:5,7,8,9)**

> *Whom can I nourish today, Jesus, Bread of Life?*

A computerized and clean commute

New York subway riders may have reason to feel a bit jealous of Europeans who ride the Metro.

Lyons, France, has the world's first completely automated subway — there are no conductors at all. A computer controls the command system and infrared lights stop the train if someone or something falls onto the tracks.

Since there are no conductors' booths, riders can stand at the window in the front of the first car and enjoy a thrilling ride. Undercover train personnel walk around the cars in case there are problems.

Besides being cleaner than New York's famed subway system, the Lyons Metro has a 95 percent on-time rate.

The people who helped to create this subway are using their God-given gifts and talents. Advances in technology can help to make the world a better place.

You received without paying, give without pay. (Matthew 10:8)

Help me to give freely of the gifts and talents You've given me at no cost, Creator.

Many Marthas, many gifts

A group of women give new meaning to the term "recycling."

The Martha Group at St. Bridget Parish in River Falls, Wisconsin, meets once a month for five hours.

Everything they use is not only recycled and donated, it's whatever would have been thrown away.

They piece together patchwork quilts for homeless people in the fall.

Newborns' layettes, bibs, washcloths and toys are made in spring and fall. Booties and sweaters are also knit.

Christmas boxes are prepared for the residents of two local nursing homes.

In five hours, once a month, discarded materials get a second lease on life. Only cloth diapers for the layettes have to be bought.

It's amazing what can be done in so little time for so little money to make this world a little better.

Do good, and lend, expecting nothing in return. Your reward will be great, and you will be children of the Most High. (Luke 6:35)

Jesus, I want to be a generous child of the Father today.

Philanthropy of compassion

A former Christopher staff member, Charles Ascenzi, now deceased, was an unusually kind, nonjudgmental person.

Another staff member was with Charles one day when he was approached by a shabby panhandler. The man told a wildly improbable tale of woe, but Charles gave him $10.

After the panhandler left, the other staff member said to Charles, "You shouldn't have given that man money. The story he told couldn't have been true. He just made it up."

"Yes," said Charles, "but imagine how it would feel to be so desperate you *had* to make up a story like that."

Charles chose not to judge the man's behavior, but to show compassion for his need.

With the judgment you pronounce you will be judged. (Matthew 7:2)

Teach me to be kind and nonjudgmental, Jesus.

Pass along your past

Do you remember the stories your parents and grandparents told you about the days of their youth? Telling stories is a great way to preserve your family history and open the doors of communication.

Sue Chevalier, a writer for Knight-Ridder Newspapers, suggests a few ways to share the times of your life with your own children:

● Bring your kids to one of your childhood places, and relate a memorable event that occurred there.

● Share your memories while you whip up a special snack.

● Repeat favorite stories over time so that your kids will remember them and pass them on to the next generation.

This is one way that you can communicate with your children, and maybe even their children.

The good leave an inheritance to their children's children. (Proverbs 13:22)

Father, enable us to leave an inheritance for our children's children by recounting our family's history.

Teens, gangs, and families

The very mention of teenage gangs strikes terror into the hearts of parents. Since the '80s, gangs have become more violent. Today, they're armed with guns and often involved in drug traffic, robbery, even murder.

Why do teens join gangs? Most of them say it's for a feeling of self-esteem, of belonging, of having someone who cares about them. Parents may work long hours and have little time to spend with their children. Youngsters often turn to gangs for the emotional support lacking at home.

To keep young people out of gangs, counselors advise parents: Encourage your children to take part in wholesome activities. Spend time with them. Set a good example for them. And above all, let them know that they are loved.

I will heal their faithlessness; I will love them freely, for My anger has turned from them. (Hosea 14:4)

Compassionate and loving Lord, make parents compassionate and loving with all their children but especially the most difficult.

Homeless but talented folks perform

The master of ceremonies began a talent show in New York City recently by saying, "Life is hard, but it can be sweet. Where you are today, you don't have to be tomorrow. You are somebody."

The contestants were homeless people from a drop-in shelter near Grand Central Station. Their audience included homeless and formerly homeless people and neighborhood business people.

These shows are held regularly. They provide entertainment for people whose lives include few luxuries.

They also help dispel negative stereotypes by showing business people that there are talented and employable people who are homeless.

But most importantly, the shows give the homeless new hope by making them feel good about themselves.

I delivered the poor who cried, and the fatherless who had none to help. (Job 29:12)

Jesus, I want to help poor people by dispelling negative stereotypes about them. Help me.

Hard talk, soft words

Sometimes we have to have conversations with people that we know are going to be difficult. You can improve your chances for not inflicting more stress than necessary on yourself or the other person by following these tips from Christine Leatz, author of "Career Success/Personal Stress":

● Start with some point of agreement. Finding common ground is important, even if you have to dig for it.

● Say "and" not "but." "But" negates the value of anything you've said before it in the sentence.

● Limit the number of times you say "you" — it can make the other person feel criticized. Instead, use "I" to let your listener know how you think and feel. "I" also minimizes defensiveness and boosts communication.

Whatever you say, think first.

Let your speech always be gracious, seasoned with salt, so that you may know how you ought to answer everyone. (Colossians 4:6)

Season my speech with grace and gentleness, Word of the Father.

Clown calms fears

When Hurricane Andrew hit southern Florida in 1992, it destroyed homes and businesses and terrified many youngsters who didn't quite understand what had happened. They were scared by the force of the storm and the darkness and destruction that ensued.

One woman eased the children's fears. Marcela Murad is a professional clown who goes by the name of Mama Clown. She went around the tent cities that were created for the newly homeless families and entertained the children with jokes, songs and magic tricks. Her clowning helped some of the little ones relax. As Ms. Murad put it, "My satisfaction is to know I was able to put a smile on children's faces and make them act like kids again."

Is there a way you can help someone overcome a fear?

The Lord said . . . 'Do not fear or be dismayed.' (Joshua 8:1)

Courageous God, how can I help someone conquer a particularly disabling fear?

Little letter makes big difference

Workers at a Federal District Court noticed that nobody from Hartford, Connecticut, had served on a Federal grand jury for the past three years. When they checked, they found that their computer records listed everybody in Hartford as dead.

The name of the city had been entered in the wrong place. As a result, the "d" at the end of "Hartford" had run over into the column giving the status of prospective jurors. And "d" was the computer code for "Dead."

On computer records, wrong placement of one letter killed off a whole city.

On the positive side, too, little things can make a big difference. One person's writing to a congressman can help spark needed legislation. One vote can determine the outcome of an election.

A little yeast leavens the whole batch of dough. (Galatians 5:9)

When I'm discouraged, Holy Spirit, remind me that, literally, every little bit helps to make this a more human, humane and holy world.

Move on from failure

We all fail in our lives. The problem, however, is not the failure, but how we deal with it. Here are some suggestions that may help you:

Stop acting like a failure.

Keep your sense of humor.

Remember, God says you are a success and He forgives your failure.

Do not relive and dwell on your failure.

Share your feelings of failure with someone who can give you emotional support and feedback.

Recall how many Biblical people achieved great things for God AFTER they had failed: David after he'd committed adultery, Peter after he'd denied Jesus.

As Teresa of Avila said, "Who has God lacks nothing." Including the ability to rise and try again.

Who is a God like You, pardoning iniquity and passing over transgression . . . because He delights in steadfast love. (Micah 7:18)

As You pardon me, Forgiving Lord, so may I pardon myself.

Making the most of talents

Mary Lou Retton, the first American woman to win an Olympic gold medal in gymnastics, said:

"We are each put on this earth to make a particular contribution to humanity. Some as teachers; others as housewives, executives, athletes, doctors, farmers . . . The list is endless. Although God . . . has a plan for every one of us, he gives us choices. It is our responsibility to make the best of those choices in order to achieve our ultimate purpose.

"God gave me a talent to do gymnastics. But I had to choose to . . . dedicate . . . years of my life to the sport . . . to make the most of that talent."

Your talent may not be as conspicuous as this Olympian's athletic ability, but that doesn't mean it's less important. Use your special gifts well.

All these (gifts) are inspired by one and the same Spirit, who apportions to each one individually as He wills. (1 Corinthians 12:11)

Generous Father, enable me to appreciate the talents You've given me — and use them well.

Encompassing spirituality

Native American cultures have much to teach us.

Native Americans have long been aware of the need to respect the earth. And they stress sharing and working together.

Underlying these attitudes is the spirituality that pervades their lives. They have no word for religion because they make no distinction between the religious and the secular.

An anthropologist said of Native Americans in California, "The life of these Indians is nothing but a continuous religious experience."

Whatever our religion, we can make it a part of our everyday lives. We can open our eyes to the beauty of God in the earth and the people around us. And we can make each daily task a prayer when we seek to live in harmony with God's will.

If you will, you can keep the commandments, and to act faithfully is a matter of your own choice. (Sirach 15:15)

Enable me, Holy Spirit, to choose the right, the way of the commandments, the way of life.

God's generous hand

Iris Turner and her husband had four small children and a tight budget. A decision to tithe — tax themselves a fixed percentage every week or month to give to church or charity — made it even tighter.

When an ad announced a sale on boys' winter jackets, Mrs. Turner rushed to buy two. They weren't washable. She put them back, reluctantly. But her sons still needed jackets.

Outside the store Mrs. Turner dropped a quarter in a Salvation Army kettle and received a pamphlet in return.

The pamphlet on tithing reinforced the Turners' decision to continue, despite the hardships it imposed.

Later, a neighbor called to say she had found two of her sons' outgrown jackets while cleaning out closets. And . . . could the Turners use them?

They were perfect fits. Washable, too.

God is never outdone in generosity. Be generous to Him in whatever ways you can.

The measure you give will be the measure you get. (Mark 4:24)

Magnanimous God, how can I be magnanimous with You and with my sisters and brothers who are most in need?

Reflections on the Lord's Prayer

A friend of The Christophers wrote to tell us how one day she stopped to really think about the Lord's Prayer.

"Our Father who art in heaven . . . If we dare to call You Father Who is just and good," reflects Doris Wood, "we must prove by our lives that the kinship is real. Good comes from good and just comes from just . . . Since this makes us sons and daughters of the Heavenly Father, then we are all brothers and sisters."

The writer then considers modern problems in terms of the prayer: from the not-in-my-backyard attitude of not wanting low-income housing or AIDS hospices in our neighborhoods to the evils of war and neglect of the elderly.

For almost two thousand years the essential wisdom and truth of the Lord's Prayer has continued to both comfort and challenge all who address Our Father.

Take the time to reflect for yourself.

Forgive, if you have anything against any one; so that your Father . . . in heaven may forgive you your trespasses. (Mark 11:25)

Our Father who art in heaven, make me Your child in deed as well as in word.

Out of ignorance, a message

Legendary soul singer James Brown has had some ups and downs in his lifetime. He even spent 2 years in prison on assault and weapons convictions.

But while visiting students at the Webster Academy in Oakland, California, he had only one message for them: stay in school.

Brown told the kids, "The worst killer in the world . . . is ignorance. With all the success I've had, I've been broke four times because of ignorance." He emphasized that education is the key to success. "There's nothing that can take the place of knowledge," he said.

Education is important for everyone — and your education doesn't end when you finish school. Try to keep up a lifetime of learning.

Wisdom teaches her children and gives help to those who seek her. (Sirach 4:11)

Holy Spirit, give success to my pursuit of Your wisdom.

Brake that fall into anger

The elevator isn't new. Lifts have been used in construction from the time the pyramids were built. But they were too dangerous for passengers. Cables could break — with disastrous results.

Then in 1854, Elisha Otis of Vermont found a way to make elevators safe. His invention used a large compressed spring. If the elevator cable went slack, this spring automatically snapped out, pushing two iron bars into notched guide rails in the elevator shaft. This locked the elevator in place, protecting passengers.

When our temper snaps and anger gets out of control, the results can also be disastrous. We can't help feeling angry at times, but we can put a "safety lock" on what we say or do. When we keep anger in check, nobody gets hurt.

> **Refrain from anger, and forsake wrath! Fret not yourself; it tends only to evil.**
> **(Psalm 37:8)**

Help us keep our anger in check, patient Lord who knew anger but so often checked it.

From good hearts — generosity

You may have heard of Percy Ross, the million-aire who writes the syndicated column, "Thanks A Million." The philanthropist gives away money and expensive items to people in need.

Thousands write to him each week requesting money for operations, repairs, washing machines, cars — you name it. He is 75 years old and plans to give away all of his estimated $20 million before he dies.

Mr. Ross gives away his money because he knows that there are others who need it more. And he doesn't do it anonymously because he feels people should be able to identify a good deed with a person.

"I'm not doing this for myself," he says. "I'm representing everyone who has a good heart." And you can give of yourself, out of your good heart, to those in need.

Religion that is pure and undefiled before God . . . is this: to visit orphans and widows in their affliction, and to keep oneself unstained from the world. (James 1:27)

Father of the poor, inspire my generosity.

Get ahead — with others

The next time you catch sight of a flock of geese flying overhead you might remember these facts.

Because each goose creates an uplift for the bird following by flapping its wings, the whole flock increases its flying range by 71 percent over a bird flying alone. Whenever a goose leaves the "V" formation, it feels the extra resistance of trying to fly alone. That encourages it to get back into formation.

People have a lesson to learn from those high-flying birds. We all get where we're going more easily when we accept the help of those around us and when we extend it to others.

One last fact: the geese in the back of the formation honk to encourage the others to keep up their speed. Encouragement is something we humans need to give and receive if we want to get anywhere.

Encourage him. (2 Samuel 11:25)

Encourage me, Lord, even as I try to encourage others.

"Lethal cuisine" and lifestyle

The Wall Street Journal boasted this eye-catching headline one day: "Lethal Cuisine Takes High Toll in Glasgow." But it wasn't a story about poison or pollution contaminating a food supply.

Rather, the article talked about the poor health of much of the population in what is called the "West's Sickest City." Research shows that "for lifestyle related disease, Glasgow is in a class of its own. People are literally eating and smoking themselves to death."

Coronary rates are 800 percent higher than in Japan and life expectancy is six years less than in the U.S. It is the world's lung cancer leader. Eating fats and sweets, smoking and drinking alcohol all add to the toll. Poverty, cultural habits and the environment contribute too.

Take a moment to think about your own habits.

Fear the Lord, and turn away from evil. It will be healing to your flesh. (Proverbs 3:7-8)

How can my habits, my life-style, even my health habits, reflect my respect for You and Your commandments, Creator?

Holy pictures that touch hearts

Mila Mina, a 65-year-old Byzantine icon paint-er, travels the country for nine months of the year giving her talent back to God by painting icons, special religious paintings, for churches.

As is usual with icon painters, she prepares for her painting by fasting and prayer. Then she goes to work, often for 14 hours a day, seven days a week.

Her icons are usually painted on canvas and then glued to the church wall. Subjects include scenes from the life of Jesus, saints, and the Holy Trinity.

In return Mila Mina asks only for the cost of her art supplies and her travel expenses. Quoting her father she says, ". . . if God gives you a tal-ent you give it back to Him."

We can not all paint icons, but each of us has at least one talent that we can give to God by using it.

I will make melody to the Lord, the God of Israel. (Judges 5:3)

At least I can sing to You, Source of all good things.

Of sun and summer and flowers

What plant has been described as the "original sun worshipper"? . . . been used to decorate galvanized watering cans? . . . was grown in front of prairie pioneers' sod houses? . . . has become the model for museum quality dishes? . . . turns up in greengrocers' flower displays as well as in yards and vases?

Hint. Baseball players munch its dried seeds. Kansas has made it the state flower. And edible oil is pressed from its seeds.

Of course, it's the sunflower. Yes, that sometimes ragged, weedy plant or stunningly tall one with the round, smiling, yellow heads on seemingly too thin stems.

If you think about it, sunflowers remind us of the infinite beauty of creation smiling even in August's shimmering heat.

> **Consider the lilies . . . they neither toil nor spin; yet I tell you, even Solomon in all his glory was not arrayed like one of these. (Luke 12:27)**

> *Gracious God, thank You for the beauty of all creation, including myself.*

Real kindness, real star

One day while Shira Susman was driving on a busy Los Angeles street, her car broke down. She was very nervous because her two small children were in the car with her, and she wanted to get them out to safety. But many people were driving fast and honking at them.

Suddenly, a stranger began to help by pushing Mrs. Susman's car to the side of the road. The benevolent stranger turned out to be actor Michael Keaton, best known to millions of movie fans as "Batman."

Mrs. Susman was so impressed by his unsolicited kindness that she sent a letter to the L.A. Times. She wrote, ". . . (Michael) Keaton is not like the rest of us; he is better than many of us. Thank you, Mr. Keaton, for your example."

A simple act of kindness can make someone's day.

Hold fast to love and justice, and wait continually for your God. (Hosea 12:6)

As You know, Jesus, it isn't always easy to be kind, to be just, to love. But with Your grace everything is possible.

He puts a candle in the window

Michael Richards has run a settlement house, written a book on social and ecological matters and directed a social services agency. But 24 years ago he was an unemployed, homeless 18-year-old.

Richards put his experiences together in 1991 and began "A Candle in the Window" to help the homeless, especially homeless mothers.

Located in a small apartment in New York City's Greenwich Village section, "A Candle in the Window" supplies The Body Shop and the Tweeds catalog with candles and candle holders.

Richards doesn't aim to provide the homeless with a career but with "enough to get their own apartment," and break their downward spiral.

You too can light the candle of hope — today.

What does the Lord require of you but to do justice, and to love kindness, and to walk humbly with your God. (Micah 6:8)

What can I do to light one candle of hope today, Mighty One?

Happy birthdays — and many thanks

In Japan, on a boy's 13th birthday, he takes time to remember the many ways that others have helped him.

On this birthday, a Japanese boy traditionally receives a kite with his name on it. His friends and relatives join in making a cord for the kite. They knot together string, with each person tying on a separate piece.

Before the boy flies his new kite, he looks at each knot on the cord, thinking of the person who tied it. Silently he gives thanks for all the things that person has done for him.

Any birthday would be a good time to remember what others have done for us. We often take their help for granted.

Don't forget to say "Thank you."

Always and for everything (give) thanks in the name of our Lord Jesus Christ to God the Father. (Ephesians 5:20)

Indeed, Lord, thank You for all I am and have, all that You've given me and especially thank You for Your Son.

Find a way to say "No"

If you find it difficult to say "No," you have lots of company. Most of us were raised to be agreeable, and obliging others' requests is part of it. But some demands are unreasonable, or simply too much for our own well-being.

Here are some strategies from writer Jo Coudert:

● Buy yourself some time. Many requests don't have to be answered immediately. Tell the person you'll think about it. Then you have time to consider your answer.

● Start with a compliment. Let the person know you appreciate being asked before you refuse.

● Accentuate the positive. For example: "That's an excellent offer, but we're not in a position to take advantage of it right now."

● Be courteous and direct. Say: "Sorry, but that's not something I do."

Honesty and kindness do count.

Have unity of spirit, sympathy, love for one another, a tender heart, and a humble mind. (1 Peter 3:8)

Fill me with Your own gracious, positive, tender, forgiving, humble Spirit, Jesus.

Like yourself, like others

People sometimes ask, "Isn't it more important how you feel about others than how you feel about yourself?" The two can't be separated. To be free to love others, you must like yourself.

When you like yourself, you don't need to spend your time and energy worrying about the impression you're making. You're free to take an interest in other people.

When you like yourself, you don't do things for others just to make *yourself* feel worthwhile. You're free to do things for others out of genuine concern for *them*.

When you like yourself, you don't feel that you're letting God down because you're not perfect. You're free to accept the love of God, who made you and delights in you.

> **My compassion grows warm and tender. I will not execute My fierce anger . . . for I am God and not man. (Hosea 11:8-9)**

> *Compassionate God, enable us to take as much delight in ourselves as You do.*

Fruits of memories

The late William Di Paola and his wife Bene-detta had memories of picking fresh figs "on the terraced limestone slopes of Formia," Italy. So when they emigrated and William Di Paola began his tree nursery he planted an Italian Purple Red fig tree in a barrel.

That was 23 years ago. The Di Paolas have died, but their memory bears fruit in that fig tree. Its branches are like sturdy arms raised to the sky.

Says their son Chris, "This is Pop's tree . . . To me a fig tree is like a woman . . . It's graceful; it produces."

Chris Di Paola and his brother Bill still run their father's tree nursery which has become an international exchange for the varieties of fig trees.

And there will be the usual first harvest of figs in June; another beginning mid-August.

Memories can be fruitful — and not just in figs.

Remember the wonderful works He has done. (Psalm 105:5)

May the remembrance of Your goodness fill me with gratitude, Loving Father.

Virtue's reward

Here are some encouraging thoughts on virtue from the pen of Elizabeth Gaskell.

"People may talk . . . about the little respect that is paid to virtue . . . but in the long run, true virtue always has its proportionate reward in the respect and reverence of everyone whose esteem is worth having.

"To be sure, it is not rewarded after the way of the world as mere worldly possessions are . . . But all the better and more noble qualities in the hearts of others make ready and go forth to meet (virtue) on its approach — provided only it be pure, simple, unconscious of its own existence."

The Apostle James advised us to show by our good lives that our works are done with "gentleness born of wisdom." The virtuous life then is proof of genuine wisdom.

> **Who is wise and understanding among you? Show by your good life that your works are done with gentleness born of wisdom. (James 3:13)**

> *Come Holy Spirit, make me truly wise.*

When you hear the beep

To find out how suburban teenagers spend their time, 75 teenagers were given beepers on belts. For several months, every time the beepers sounded, the teens wrote down what they were doing, who they were with, and what their feelings were. The findings were reported in a book entitled *Being Adolescent.*

Theodore Sizer, an education professor at Brown University, commented on two facts that emerged: The teenagers spent surprisingly little time with adults and they spent a lot of time alone. Professor Sizer said, "The biggest distress of kids growing up today is caused by adults — we neglect them."

The time we spend with young people is the most precious gift we can give them.

> **(Let us not neglect) to meet together ... encouraging one another. (Hebrews 10:25)**

> *Enlighten us when we are with teens, Child of Nazareth, so that we will be able to encourage them.*

More than a job

In a difficult economy with a lot of people out of work, it isn't enough to ask "what kind of job do you want?" People need to use all their resources to find work, especially work that has a special meaning for them.

But even if the job you get, or already have, is less than your dream career, it's worth far more than just putting food on the table and paying your rent.

Every job can make a difference. Each of us makes our daily work more than the sum of its tasks. Ask Tommy Maher, a Boston bartender. Over the years he has raised thousands of dollars for hospitalized children. He's bought equipment for disabled youngsters and brought athletes to visit their bedsides. And he's done it by involving his customers in his cause.

He sums up: "I think people should be more than bartenders or plumbers or whatever they may be. I think we have to do more than just work for a living. We have to give."

You do well if you really fulfill the royal law according to the scripture, 'You shall love your neighbor as yourself.' (James 2:8)

Inform my efforts to put my love of neighbor into action, Holy Spirit.

1,000 miles to spread the word

Jeannette Goodman is the mother of a 32-year-old mentally ill son. She was afraid of what might happen if she was no longer able to take care of him. So she began a 1,000 mile walk from Texas to California in order to raise awareness about the homeless and mentally ill.

She packed her things into a three-wheeled "baby jogger" and hit the road. She averaged 10 miles a day, walking through the deserts of New Mexico and Arizona. She refused any donations and urged the people she met along the way to give to mental health associations or the Salvation Army. Her goal is to form a council that would provide private funding for the homeless and mentally ill.

Jeannette Goodman is concerned about her child but she realizes that all homeless and mentally ill people are somebody's children, too. We can do our bit to help solve the problems of today so that tomorrow may be a better place for all our children.

Hate evil, and love good, and establish justice. (Amos 5:15)

Dear Lord, what one thing can I do or what one word can I say, today, that will make the world more humane?

Some food, some comfort, some normal life

In late August, 1992, Hurricane Andrew roared across parts of southern Florida.

Even as whole palm trees whizzed past, restaurateur Jack Valenti knew he had to open for dinner. "These people won't be able to feed themselves," he thought.

On the same circuit as the local hospital, he had electricity the next day and became one of the first places "where people could compare losses, share sympathies, forget the havoc."

Valenti made up to 25 calls for supplies, used Evian water for cooking, overpaid for Pepsi, but didn't raise food prices.

A customer said that eating at Valenti's had made her feel "the world is right again."

You can always make the world right again for someone.

Be merciful, even as your Father is merciful. (Luke 6:36)

How can I make the world right again for someone, God?

Racing toward peace

Mirsada Buric is a 22-year-old Olympic runner from Bosnia. The young woman trained for the Olympics by running through the war-torn streets of what used to be Yugoslavia.

She would wait for the air raid sirens to wail, and then dart through the streets, dodging sniper bullets. She was almost hit twice by gunfire, but continued to run daily. At the 1992 summer games in Barcelona, her mind was not on the gold, but on the fate of her family back home.

Ms. Buric said, "I'm just grateful to be here, because I think it is the greatest honor to represent a newly independent country that is trying to survive . . . I just wish I could see the day when the fighting will stop."

Hopefully, we will all see the day when there will be world peace. Pray and do your part.

> **As you have done, it shall be done to you, your deeds shall return on your own head. (Obadiah 15)**

> *When we are tempted to violence, Author of Peace, remind us that those who use the sword will fall by the sword. And too many who are innocent are cut down also.*

Stories of ourselves

Every family has its share of family stories. Stories about itself. Stories that offer a sense of continuity each time they are told. And in many homes they are told often, much to the chagrin of the children who profess boredom, or embarrassment — if the anecdote is about them.

Nevertheless they offer great value. Life magazine editor Roger Rosenblatt says, "our stories are our epics — quite insignificant to history, but all the world to us . . . Some tales are more interesting than others, because they reflect how mysterious are the relationships we form as a family — accidents that give us our whole lives."

And that is probably how it has been as long as families have gathered and talked and passed along stories of themselves. Hopefully, it always will be.

> **When your children ask their parents . . . 'What do these stones mean?' then you shall let your children know, 'Israel passed over this Jordan on dry ground.' (Joshua 4:21-22)**

> *Enable families to tell their stories of faith and love from one generation to another, Blessed Lord.*

Work of mercy, holiness

Do you ever think of your job as part of your spiritual life? Many people probably consider their daily tasks the way they earn their living rather than their way to holiness. In fact, work is both.

According to Dorothy Day, co-founder of the Catholic Worker movement: "All work, whether building, increasing food production, running credit unions, working in factories . . . all these things can come under the heading of works of mercy."

Each person's job offers opportunities to nourish the soul as well as to put food on the table. It means not just doing a good day's work, but looking out for the "other guy" — customer and co-worker, supervisor and subordinate. And it means accepting ourselves and others as human beings, capable of mistakes and of wonderful possibilities.

> **Whatever your task, put yourselves into it, as done for the Lord and not for your masters . . . Masters treat your slaves justly and fairly, for you . . . also have a Master in heaven. (Colossians 3:23;4:1)**

> *Holy Spirit, ever at work in the world, improve employee — employer relations.*

What are your personal ethics?

Here are some tips for ethical living from the International Coordinating Committee on Religion and the Earth.

Ethical living means that . . .

● we meet current needs while keeping the ability of future generations to meet their needs in mind;

● all human beings are entitled to the basic necessities of life;

● all are able to participate in a sustainable society through legal and corporate structures;

● conflict is resolved through consultation, not conflict;

● we live frugally, simply, with inner freedom;

● all are able to develop physically, intellectually, morally and spiritually.

One decision at a time. One day at a time. Ethical living, moral living, is possible.

If you had walked in the way of God, you would be dwelling in peace for ever. Learn (therefore) where there is wisdom . . . strength . . . understanding . . . length of days and life. (Baruch 3:13-14)

Open my eyes to the wisdom of Your law, Law-Giver of Sinai.

Churches extend practical help

Economic problems and unemployment are taking their toll on the lives of many people. While there are no simple or quick answers, churches across the land are coming up with ways to help their members and neighbors.

In White Bear Lake, Minnesota, the First Lutheran Church and St. Mary of the Lake host a cooperative support group. In one year, 90 men and women found jobs through the program.

Meanwhile, a career planner from the University of Maryland conducts job transition workshops in her parish. Another church offers a job bank through its bulletin. And St. Margaret's Catholic Church and Bel Air United Methodist operate a joint food bank venture.

Think about your own church. Maybe your leadership could offer fresh hope to friends and neighbors who need a hand.

If a brother and sister is ill-clad and in lack of daily food, and one of you says to them, 'Go in peace, be warmed and filled,' without giving them the things needed . . . what does it profit? (James 2:15-16)

Giving hope to needy brothers and sisters is often difficult, Father. Encourage us when the going gets tough.

Compulsive — and young — gamblers

"Compulsive Gambling among teens is not only growing, it's becoming the addiction of the nineties," according to Valerie Lorenz, director of Baltimore's Compulsive Gambling Center.

Why are young people susceptible to this addiction? Experts say that a desire to experiment, lack of self-control and low self-esteem contribute to the problem.

If a parent senses that a youngster is in trouble, if money is missing, if a lot of lottery stubs are around, the child needs to be approached. While few groups or treatment centers exist that concentrate on young compulsive gamblers, local mental health agencies can help. And so can Gamblers Anonymous.

Like many addictions, gambling is hard to deal with, but recovery is possible. It's the best chance you'll ever take.

> **The grace of God has appeared, bringing salvation to all, training us to . . . live lives that are self-controlled, upright, and godly. (Titus 2:11-12)**

> *Enable us, Jesus, to accept the grace necessary to overcome addictions.*

A woman of substance

Nurse's aide Sylvia Babitch of Shirley, New York, won nearly two million dollars. Suddenly she was financially independent. She could do whatever she wanted to do — retire . . . travel.

What she chose to do was to go on working as a nurse's aide at a home for the chronically ill. Her life revolves around her patients there. She said, "We become their family. We want to give them the love they're missing."

Her patients return the affection. One of them said, "I don't know what I'd do without her."

With her newfound wealth, Ms. Babitch bought some good sneakers to wear at work — and a convertible. But she doesn't want to leave her job.

The warmth and dedication she brings to her work make a real difference in the lives of others.

Make love your aim. (1 Corinthians 14:1)

Jesus, love was the aim of Your life. May love be the aim of my life, too.

High cost of courage

Wallace, Louisiana, had lost thousands of oil and chemical industry jobs in the last decade. Then it was chosen to be the site of the world's largest wood pulp and rayon plant.

Local residents, environmentalists and preservationists unified. They gathered emissions statistics. 8,000 tons of hardwood would be cut daily. 16 billion gallons of waste water discharged into the Mississippi River yearly.

The coalition harried the Environmental Protection Agency. They reminded everyone that the Mississippi provided drinking water for downstream cities.

Only 1,000 full-time jobs and 800 temporary ones had been promised.

The coalition won. Wallace's environment, and the Mississippi were spared this additional pollution. 1,800 jobs were sacrificed. Local unemployment remains high.

Courage is frequently painful. It's also admirable.

> **Let us make a covenant with our God . . . and let it be done according to law. Arise . . . be strong and do it. (Ezra 10:3-4)**

> *Come, Holy Spirit, come with Your gift of fortitude.*

Consider the good

The pews and confessionals of our churches are full of people who don't see themselves as they are. Or, as God sees them for that matter.

Asked, "What can you say that's good about yourself?" they hesitate. They may recall some very real sins. But it is usually difficult for them to remember how hard they're trying — trying to live a life of love, compassion and service toward God and their neighbors.

Sir Alec Guinness played Pope Innocent III in the movie, "Brother Sun, Sister Moon." At one point he stoops to kiss Francis of Assisi's bare feet. He says, "Francesco, Francesco. In our obsession with original sin, we do often forget original innocence." We *are* redeemed creatures!

What can you say that's good about yourself? A great deal.

> **What are human beings that You are mindful of them, mortals that You care for them? You have made them a little lower than God. (Psalm 8:4-5)**

> *Never permit me to forget, Creator, that You created human beings in Your image and came to us in love through Your Son, Jesus the Christ.*

One creative manager

For a supervisor or employer, group leader or coach, bringing out the best in others is important to the success of the individual and the team. It requires understanding. As Joe McCarthy, manager of the New York Yankees during the 30's and 40's demonstrated, it calls for creativity.

One day, he approached his shortstop Frank Crosetti, saying, "I'm not satisfied with the way Lou Gehrig is playing first base. He's too lackadaisical. I want you to help me. From now on, charge every ball. When you get it, fire it as quickly and as hard as you can to first base . . . Throw it fast and make it tough for him."

Later, a coach commented to McCarthy, "I guess you were trying to wake up Gehrig."

The manager responded, "There wasn't a thing wrong with Gehrig. Crosetti was the one who was sleeping. I wanted to wake up Crosetti."

Watch therefore — for you do not know when the master of the house will come . . . lest he . . . find you asleep. (Mark 13:35,36)

Help me be alert to the signs of the times, Merciful Savior.

Old belief points in wrong direction

There's an old belief that if you're lost, you can figure out directions from the moss on trees, since it grows only on the north side.

Unfortunately, this is not true.

A tree growing on dry, level ground with no other trees close to it may have moss just on the north side of the trunk. But a tree growing on low ground or in a dense forest is more likely to have moss on all sides.

Basing a decision on the false belief about where moss grows will just lead a confused hiker further astray. Wise hikers will have a properly oriented compass to guide them.

In any situation, our decisions need to be based on accurate information and sound principles. Only then can we make the right choices.

You are my lamp, O Lord, and my God lightens my darkness. (2 Samuel 22:29)

Holy Wisdom, give us the light of Your wisdom in every situation.

Putting dreams to work

Here's the story of one woman who wanted to turn a dream into a reality for herself and her family.

Romana Banuelos married, had two children, divorced and left her native Mexico to support her family by working at an El Paso laundry — all by the time she was 18.

She went to her aunt in Los Angeles, arriving with her last seven dollars. She took a job washing dishes in a restaurant. While she saved money, she watched and learned the business. Ms. Banuelos started making and selling tortillas.

Eventually Romana's Mexican Food Products became a large corporation. More than that, to help the people of her community, she helped start a bank.

In time, Romana Banuelos became the thirty-fourth Treasurer of the United States.

Where only failure might have been predicted, success flourished. Attitude can mean everything.

I can do all things in Him who strengthens me. (Philippians 4:13)

Be my strength, God my Rock.

A time to reap

Here are some thoughts from a French pastor, Philippe Zeissig, on life and time and aging.

"Perhaps you have walked through a field which has just been harvested. The grain had been reaped; all that remained were the stalks, cut within a few inches of the soil; the clods of earth; and the inevitable weeds sprouting up.

"Our life isn't always where we think it is. We must say, as of the harvested field: the crop isn't there any more, it's in the barn, it's somewhere else . . .

"This life, which seems lost amid the afflictions of old age, isn't wasted: it is the harvested field. This life is elsewhere, in the memory and the heart of God."

Those words are a necessary and beautiful reminder: our lives are not defined only by who and what we are now, but by where we have been before and how we have lived our days.

The Son of Man is to come with His angels in the glory of His Father, and then He will repay everyone for what has been done. (Matthew 16:27)

Jesus, give us that patient endurance necessary to win the reward of everlasting life.

Fresh answers to life's questions

We may say, "Kids say the darnedest things." But sometimes, youngsters say the wisest things.

Steve and Ruth Bennett surveyed 300 kids aged 4 to 6 years old, and compiled the funniest and most intriguing responses in their book, "Kids' Answers to Life's Big Questions."

Some big problems that adults have are answered with only the wisdom a child could have. For example, what is the best way to make a friend? One child said, "Share dinosaur toys and go for a walk." And if someone is working too hard, or upset about work, what should they do? One youngster suggested, "Stop work, go outside and take a long walk in a meadow."

Children can teach us a great deal with their innocence. Perhaps your kids will share their wisdom with you, if you listen.

> **Truly . . . whoever does not receive the kingdom of God like a child shall not enter it. (Mark 10:15)**

> *How can I imitate the best qualities of a little child, Babe in the manger?*

Of ice cream and dreams

People in Harlem, New York, are able to enjoy a new ice cream shop thanks to the kindness and innovative thinking of some business people.

Ben & Jerry's, the popular Vermont-based ice cream makers, waived its $25,000 franchise fee for Joe Holland, a businessman from Harlem. Mr. Holland gave up his lucrative law practice in 1982 to counsel homeless people. In 1986, he founded HARKhomes, a shelter for homeless men. The Ben & Jerry's store will be staffed by formerly homeless people and 75 percent of the profits will go to HARKhomes.

Joe Holland and the people at Ben & Jerry's are living examples of kindness. The ice cream company was kind to Mr. Holland, and he in turn was kind to the people in his community. Is there a way you can spread some kindness in your neighborhood?

Let justice roll down like waters, and righteousness like an ever-flowing stream. (Amos 5:24)

Remind us, Just Judge, that the way to "spread some kindness" in our neighborhoods is to be both just and merciful.

Native pride in the aloha state

A forty-year-old mother of three is leading a renewal of interest in the heritage of native Hawaiians.

Hokulani Holt-Padilla wants her people to know "they have reason to be proud." Much of their culture was suppressed in the 200 years since the arrival of Westerners. So Mrs. Holt-Padilla heads a Hawaiian-language preschool, teaches the language as well as traditional dance, and lectures on Hawaiian history.

She says that "the more people understand about each other, themselves and their past, the more they're able to appreciate and exist together in harmony."

We all have the right to be proud of our heritage. Whatever our national and ethnic background, we should be able to have a true sense of those who have gone before us — for better or for worse.

It's a right that means the most when it's shared with others.

Jacob (was) the father of Joseph, the husband of Mary, of whom Jesus was born. (Matthew 1:16)

Jesus, You were not ashamed to count saints and sinners among Your human ancestors. Help me not to be ashamed of mine.

Stand in another's shoes

Frank Daily is one of the young heroes described in Barbara Lewis's book, *Kids with Courage*.

When Frank was a teenager, he was riding a bus home from school one icy day and a pregnant woman in stocking feet got on. The bus driver asked where her shoes were. She said she had eight children to buy shoes for and couldn't afford any for herself. But she added, "It's okay, the Lord will take care of me."

Frank looked at the shabbily dressed woman and slipped off his new Nikes. He waited until other people got off the bus, then gave her his shoes. She was crying as she thanked him.

Then she turned to the bus driver and said, "See, I told you the Lord would take care of me."

Don't hesitate to be an instrument of God's help to others.

Though He was rich, yet for your sake (Jesus Christ) became poor, so that by His poverty you might become rich. (2 Corinthians 8:9)

Redeemer, make me an instrument of Your peace.

A non-sticky situation

Chemists may finally have developed a graffiti-proof coating.

A compound now being tested forms a transparent coating that nothing seems to stick to. No paint, marker, solvent, or anything else tried so far adheres to it. If it works out, it could protect walls and buildings from being marred by graffiti.

People, too, need protection from experiences that leave ugly, negative impressions on them. We all have bad experiences. Maybe someone treats us unfairly or in some way betrays our trust.

If we dwell on these experiences and harbor resentment, they can mar our outlook on life.

We can prevent such emotional damage by forgiving. Forgiveness keeps negative feelings such as anger and resentment from sticking.

Forgive, if you have anything against anyone; so that your Father in heaven may also forgive you. (Mark 11:25)

Spirit of Wisdom, I want to be able to forgive. Help me.

Put down roots

An entrepreneur has found that there's a market for 2-inch-square containers of dirt.

His company packages soil from actual places around the United States. Some are places with odd names such as Luck (Wisconsin) and Romance (Arkansas). There's even a container with soil from all 50 states.

Maybe this soil has a nostalgic appeal. Today, families are often uprooted, as jobs take them from one part of the country to another. A packet of soil may seem a link to the town or state they left. Or maybe it's an offbeat gift.

But a better gift is to make newcomers feel at home in their *new* hometown. Get to know them. Invite them to local activities. A warm welcome will be the most welcome gift.

> 'Come, O blessed of My Father, inherit the kingdom prepared for you . . . for I was a stranger and you welcomed Me.'
> (Matthew 25:34,35)

Gracious Lord, show me how to be a welcoming person in my neighborhood and parish.

Part of the web of life

Here are insights from the International Coordinating Committee on Religion and the Earth.

● The Earth is an interdependent community of life.

● Each form of life has its own intrinsic value.

● The Earth and all forms of life embody beauty. This beauty feeds the human spirit. It inspires wonder, joy, creativity.

● Human beings are one strand within the web of life. Human beings are neither above it nor outside it. They did not weave the web of life.

● Human beings have a special responsibility to preserve life in all its diversity and integrity.

● All human beings, including future generations, have a right to a healthy environment.

We show our love for our Creator best when we live our oneness, our solidarity, with all creation.

God said to Noah . . . 'I establish My covenant with you and your descendants after you, and with every living creature . . . the birds, the cattle, and every beast of the earth.' (Genesis 9:8,9-10)

God of the covenant, Lord of creation, let us humans never forget that Your covenant of life is with all living beings, not just us.

Peers offer positive pressure

Some towns in Oklahoma and Oregon use peer pressure to fight teenage crime. Youth courts there have teenage attorneys, judges, and juries.

Any teenager can serve after taking a seven-week training program and passing a simple "bar" test. Most of these courts try only misdemeanors, but in Bend, Oregon, they also try less serious felonies such as burglaries. Sentences can be up to 50 hours of community service.

But teenage offenders find the embarrassment of being tried by peers worse than the sentences.

The system seems to work. Only 11 percent of teens convicted in these courts repeat offenses. The national average is 30 to 40 percent.

Young people can be a powerful force for good. Help them use their energy constructively.

> **Rejoice . . . while you are young . . . Follow the inclination of your heart and the desire of your eyes . . . Banish anxiety from your mind, and . . . pain from your body. (Ecclesiastes 11:9,10)**

> *Son of God, help young men and women rejoice in their youth and use their energy for the common good.*

A few words can build esteem

The Crittenton Center for Young Women and Infants in Los Angeles recently commemorated its 100th anniversary.

The center is a non-profit residential facility that provides educational and vocational training for pregnant and abused teenage girls and young mothers. The young women learn about practical skills of parenting such as diapering and feeding but they also learn that they have to put their child's needs before their own.

As executive director Sharrell Blakely put it, "Self-esteem and self-worth are difficult things to define but they definitely are the key to good parenting."

We sometimes forget that children need a little boost to their self-esteem now and then. Say a few kind words to a child you know.

> **(Jesus said) 'See that you do not despise one of these little ones; for I tell you that in heaven their angels always behold the face of My Father.' (Matthew 18:10)**

Inspire parents to boost their children's sense of self-esteem and self-worth, Holy Spirit.

Thoughts on a September sunrise

This is a meditation from Ursuline Sister Paulette Anne Ducharme.

It is just before a September sunrise . . .

"Slowly, the sun's immense golden mantle spread across the meadow revealing a field of diamonds that shimmered and sparkled. No greed could touch them nor could they be stored for another day. God's treasures, like daily bread, are not to be possessed except by the memory of the spirit. This insight is September's truth; it is the September face of God . . .

"God asks in the happenings of September, if I am willing to grow beyond where I am. Am I willing to be pruned, to be replanted and cut down so that fresh growth will come in the spring? . . .

"Now it is time to walk into this day, into the daily tasks and small duties that will accompany it. I have been blessed to be present at its birth and now because I have seen the September face of God, this day will bring me life."

You have said, 'Seek you My face.' My heart says to You, 'Your face, Lord, do I seek.' Hide not Your face from me. (Psalm 27:8)

Show me, Lord, the beauty of Your face.

Rare windfall

About seven years ago, Mr. and Mrs. Derek Haythornwhite of East Crescent, England, got a strange windfall.

They were awakened by loud banging on the roof of their house. Looking out, they saw apples falling onto the house from the sky!

Presumably the apples had been carried high into the air by a storm somewhere, then later dropped.

We often receive windfalls of a different kind, such as unexpected opportunities or help in time of need. Such godsends are just that — gifts that come to us through God's love.

It's up to us what use we make of them.

If you then . . . know how to give good gifts to your children, how much more will your Father who is in heaven give good things to those who ask Him! (Matthew 7:11)

Your gifts have made me wealthy, Generous Father. May I say 'thank You' by developing those gifts.

Of elephants and senses

Steve Kline of California made some youngsters very happy.

His 3-year-old son, Zachary, is blind. Zachary was disappointed when he went to the zoo one day and was not allowed to touch the elephants, his favorite animal. Afterwards, his father called an elephant trainer that he knew and asked if the trainer would bring an elephant to his son's preschool class for show-and-tell.

An 8½ foot tall, 4-ton Indian elephant named Tai showed up at the Frances Blend School in Hollywood, the nation's only public day school for visually-impaired children. They used their other senses to touch, smell and hear it. The children were able to go for a ride on the animal's back and to experience something that they had only dreamed of.

What can you do to help a child's dream come true?

> 'What do you want Me to do for you?' . . .
> 'My teacher, let me see again.' (Mark 10:51)

My Teacher, that I might see!

"For want of a few nails"

When Hurricane Andrew devastated sections of southern Florida, questions were raised about local building codes and the quality of housing construction.

Research by a national team of experts on wind damage concluded that "a great many people are homeless and they need not have been homeless — but for want of a few nails."

Building codes in the ravaged area require houses to withstand winds of 120 miles per hour. Many problems occurred where the code was not followed. The conclusion by the Wind Engineering Research Council: houses "need to be constructed with a high level of attention to details . . . Omissions can provide the weak link which leads to major damage."

Attention to details, to the little things of life can make a huge difference. Build your life with care.

Be careful to apply (your)selves to good deeds. (Titus 3:8)

May we, even as we are building our lives with care, remember that it is You, Lord, who have laid the foundation and put the cornerstone in place.

An apple for the stranger

Life in the big city has its ups and downs. For Frank Sweeney, falling down on the streets of New York had a definite up-side to it.

Leaving a greengrocer with a shopping bag filled with thirty apples, he tripped on a broken curb and fell into the intersection, surrounded by the apples which had tumbled from his bag.

In the time it took him to get up and dust himself off, the apples — all thirty of them — were once again resting in their sack, thanks to the quick work of half a dozen pedestrians.

The incident left the apple-buyer and his fruit barely bruised. Indeed, the New Yorker was happily surprised by the courtesy of the men and women who took a few seconds out of their day to perform a small but appreciated kindness for a stranger.

A word fitly spoken is like apples of gold in a setting of silver. (Proverbs 25:11)

In all the little ways, but especially by being kind, may I indeed love my neighbor as I love myself, Jesus.

A place of comfort

115 years after production of the Brumby rocker began in Marietta, Georgia, in 1875, it was scheduled to stop. The large chairs, distinguished by their high backs, would become a lost piece of Southern Americana.

Their popularity never waned. It was the difficulty in obtaining and repairing the production machinery and the dwindling supplies of oak and cane needed for the chairs that signaled the end.

Carole Melson heads The Rocker Shop which produced the Brumby rocker, named for the original family that made them. The comfort of the chairs is what made people enjoy them. "What's important is not just the way it looks," says Ms. Melson, "but the way it feels."

The comfort we offer each other matters a great deal.

> **Truly I tell you, just as you did it to one of the least of these who are members of My family, you did it to Me. (Matthew 25:40)**

> *Jesus, help us remember that we comfort You when we comfort the least of our sisters and brothers.*

Happy? Put others first

Most of us want to be happy. We seek fulfillment, but all too often we don't seem to find it. In fact, there is a simple way. It comes by putting the focus on other people.

Start by asking yourself, "What good can I do for someone today?" Consider all the people around you, at home, on the job, in your neighborhood. Then do something. It doesn't have to be a big favor, it can be as simple as a compliment on a job well done.

Then do something harder: be nice to a person you dislike or who dislikes you. It might be tough to do even a little thing, but positive action can help both of you.

Finally, single out a person you usually ignore and say or do something to make them feel special.

If you want to be happy yourself, be kind to others.

> **Hold unfailing your love for one another, since love covers a multitude of sins.**
> **(1 Peter 4:8)**
>
> *Spirit of the living God, how can I be kind today?*

Trading time

Here are some ideas for simplifying and enriching your life.

● If there's a library in your town, become a borrower and use other library services, too. You'll meet your neighbors and make friends.

● Watch children at play . . . sooner or later imagination takes over. The importance of imagination in even adult play is worth pondering.

● Have a sink full of dishes? Organize the family round that sink and soon everything will be clean and put away, and precious moments of family togetherness will have been found.

● Get in the habit of taking lunch. Better eating habits should result. And you'll appreciate the treat of buying lunch out once in a while.

There are many ways of simplifying your life. Moments of family togetherness should increase. The clutter of gadgets should decrease. You may save money, too.

(There is) a time for every matter under heaven. (Ecclesiastes 3:1)

Teach us, Master, to make time, to take time, to simplify our lives so as to live humanely.

Follow the tiger's trail

Faith and prayer lead to action. Anthony de Mello retold this ancient Middle-Eastern story:

A man walking in a forest saw a fox that had lost its legs, and he wondered how it survived. Then he saw a tiger come up carrying game in its mouth. The tiger ate all it wanted and then left the rest of the meat for the fox. The next day, he saw the tiger do the same thing.

The man marveled at how God provided and said, "I'll just rest and trust God to provide for me, too."

He sat waiting for days, but no food appeared and he was starving. Then he heard a voice say, "You don't understand. Stop imitating the fox and follow the example of the tiger."

Faith calls us to act — to help ourselves and to be the instrument of God's help to others.

I by my works will show you my faith. (James 2:18)

May my works, my very life, proclaim my faith, Jesus.

"Pitch in and help"

Tabor House is a residence in Hartford, Connecticut, for men who have AIDS. The house was started by Sister Laura Herold two years ago when she saw "others who still have unnecessary fears about the disease . . . turn their backs."

Tabor House has a staff of volunteers who celebrate holidays with the residents, take them out to dinner, fishing, and other activities. The house provides a home and compassion for these men who may have been shunned by others.

Joan Gallagher, assistant director, said, "AIDS is a social problem, not just an individual problem. We all could do more to pitch in and help."

Educate yourself and your children about AIDS. The better informed you are, the bigger difference you can make.

Get wisdom; get insight. (Proverbs 4:5)

Give me wisdom, Holy Spirit.

Your own wonderful life

During his illustrious acting career, James Stewart has made many memorable films. The one he considers his personal favorite is Frank Capra's "It's a Wonderful Life."

When the movie was released in 1947 it was not a box office success. Stewart believes it gained its great popularity in time because of the values it affirms: "love of hard work, love of community, love of country, and love of God."

The film tells the story of a good man facing personal disaster who gets to see what life would have been like for his loved ones if he had not been born. He learns that he has made a real difference to others.

Perhaps that's the most basic reason for the film's continuing appeal. Each one of us needs an occasional reminder that we can change the world for the better.

If you will, you can keep the commandments. (Sirach 15:15)

Enlighten and strengthen my will, God, so that by freely choosing to walk in Your way I can make this a better world.

Not just hanging out at the mall

More and more students at a Toronto high school were hanging out at a local mall instead of attending school. Resourceful educators decided to open a classroom in the mall.

This special program is designed to attract dropouts and potential dropouts. Students in it spend mornings studying marketing and "life skills." Afternoons, they work in stores and offices to get experience. The program helps keep students in school and out of trouble.

Not all communities can offer such an alternative, but there are lots of volunteer programs that reach out to young people. Big Brother and Sister programs, tutoring, and so on, help them use their talent constructively.

You can help. Be a volunteer.

Cease to do evil, learn to do good; seek justice, correct oppression; defend the fatherless, plead for the widow. (Isaiah 1:16-17)

Just Lord, how can we extend Your reign of justice?

Even experts can fall

Gibbons are considered the most agile of all animals. That's why I was surprised to learn that among these little apes, one of every four adults has broken at least one bone in accidents.

Although gibbons don't have tails, they have relatively long arms. And as they travel through the trees, they use their hands like hooks. They make long swings from branch to branch, covering as much as 25 or 30 feet in a single swing.

Yet even these champion tree-swingers fall often enough so that a quarter of the gibbon population have broken bones!

For apes and for people, failures are a fact of life. The only way to avoid them is never to do anything. Don't be discouraged by failures. Remember, they're a part of learning.

Take heart ... do not be afraid.
(Matthew 14:27)

Help me not to fear any failure except the failure to love You, Jesus.

Exchange of friendship

Holy Family School in the Bronx has a sister school of the same name in San Jose, California. After the 1989 earthquake, the New York students sent gifts and letters of encouragement to their west coast friends. Later they planned a teacher exchange program.

For Californian Susan Hensen, coming east was a bit of a culture shock. Though friends had warned her about the perils of New York, she found it warm and friendly. Ms. Hensen was welcomed by a staff volleyball game held in her honor. Students helped her make a video showing not only tourist attractions but interviews with teachers and staff.

Meanwhile, across the continent teacher Walter Lastowski taught music and staged a variety show for his adopted western school.

Friendship and understanding stretch from person to person whatever the distance.

A friend loves at all times. (Proverbs 17:17)

Bless those who are friends. May their friendship flourish, Best Friend of us all.

Woolly-bear weather

According to folklore, a thick coat of fur on bears — or various other animals — is believed to forecast a cold winter.

But naturalists say thick fur doesn't tell anything about the *coming* year. They say it tells us that the *past* year was a good one for the animal — that it's healthy and had plenty to eat.

One animal sign does seem to have a possible basis in fact. Popular belief is that the wider the brown band on woolly-bear caterpillars, the colder the winter will be. More often than not, this proves true. Naturalists don't understand why, but it does appear to be more than coincidence.

Life often seems as unpredictable as the weather. But when we trust God, we can cope. We're not paralyzed by fear about the future.

Father, into Your hands I commit my spirit! (Luke 23:46)

Yes, Abba, I do put my life in Your hands.

Religion's new welcome in Russia

A few years ago, the Arts Production Corp. of Sofrino, Russia, sold about 700,000 crosses and religious medals a month. Now it sells over 5 million.

Religion is flourishing in the former U.S.S.R. And the company which makes art objects for the many reopening Russian Orthodox churches and their members is doing a booming business.

The 1,650 workers are out of the ordinary as well. They earn far more than the standard wage, have benefits like their own grocery store and real opportunity for advancement. The work ethic and incentives are part of the routine.

From votive candles that cost pennies to gold pulpits, people are able to satisfy the needs of their liturgy, and indeed, of their hearts once more.

The Lord is a refuge to His people. (Joel 3:16)

Thank you, God, for restoring religious freedom to much of Eastern Europe. May all its people be true to You.

Prayer to the Great Spirit

Allow me to share this traditional Native American prayer with you:

"O Great Spirit whose voice I hear in the winds, and whose breath gives life to all the world, hear me! I am small and weak, I need Your strength and wisdom. Let me walk in beauty, and make my eyes ever behold the . . . sunset.

"Make my hands respect the things You have made and my ears sharp to hear Your voice. Make me wise so that I may understand the things You have taught my people. Let me learn the lessons You have hidden in every leaf and rock.

"I seek strength, not to be greater than my brother, but to fight my greatest enemy — myself.

"Make me always ready to come to You with clean hands and straight eyes. So when life fades, as the fading sunset, my spirit may come to You without shame."

Happy is the person who meditates on wisdom . . . pursuing her like a hunter, and lying in wait on her paths. (Sirach 14:20,22)

Grant me a successful pursuit of Your wisdom, Holy Spirit.

Seeking truth, exploring worlds

Back in 1947, Thor Heyerdahl of Norway fascinated the world by sailing his raft *Kon-Tiki* from Peru to Polynesia. He wanted to illustrate his theories of ancient seafarers who could have visited far-flung corners of the world.

Now in his late seventies, the explorer has returned to Peru to uncover the archeological treasures of kingdoms that existed even before the Incas. Thor Heyerdahl offered some thoughts on Columbus and the 500th anniversary of his arrival in America. The occasion should have been cause to "celebrate not only the first European who came here but also the people who stood on the shores to greet him. We should call it the Great Encounter, not the Great Discovery."

Throughout history people have dared to challenge the limits of what we know. Some of their names are familiar, most are not. But all who seek knowledge and truth deserve respect.

> **I determined to take (Wisdom) to live with me, knowing that she would give me good counsel . . . Because of her I shall have glory among the multitudes and honor in the presence of the elders.**
> **(Wisdom of Solomon 8:9,10)**
>
> *O God, Lord of mercy, give me wisdom.*

Phrases that praise

Parenting experts often ask, "Have you hugged your children today?" Yes, there's the physical hug; but then there's the verbal hug. Here are some suggested verbal hugs for your children:

"Wow!" "Super!" "You're Special!" "Outstanding!" "Excellent!" "Great!" "Good!" "Neat!" "Well Done!" "Remarkable!" "I Knew You Could Do It!" "I'm Proud of You!" "Fantastic!" "Superstar!" "Nice Work!" "Looking Good!" "You're On Top Of It!" "Beautiful!"

Are you ready for some more phrases that praise?

"You're Incredible!" "Bravo!" "You're Fantastic!" "Hurray For You!" "You're On Target!" "You're On Your Way!" "How Nice!" "How Smart!" "Good Job!" "Dynamite!" "You're Beautiful!" "You're Unique!" "Good For You!" "You're a Winner!" "Spectacular!"

And, of course, "I love you."

Have you given your children many verbal hugs today?

When given sincerely, appropriately and lovingly, such words build healthy self-esteem.

Let us love one another; for love is of God. (1 John 4:7)

Jesus, show parents how to give their children "verbal hugs."

The value of an idea

Carmen Farina taught fourth graders how to read. But her influence extended from her P.S. 29 class in Brooklyn throughout her school district and beyond.

She wanted to capture her students' attention; to get them to think and form their own opinions. So she moved away from textbooks to short stories and novels.

Not only did her students respond enthusiastically, but their reading scores also improved.

Soon other teachers were asking for her reading lists. Carmen Farina is happy with the results of her innovations. "It energizes parents, kids, teachers. Literature has helped teachers rethink what they took for granted."

How often do we take things for granted? It's so easy to keep doing things just because they've always been done. Before you just do something, decide on its value.

Understanding ... cannot be gotten for gold, and silver cannot be weighed out as its price. It cannot be valued in the gold of Ophir. (Job 28:12,15-16)

Holy Wisdom, fill me with Your priceless gifts.

Pick yourself up

During 12 years of international competition, figure-skater Paul Wylie has had a lot of falls — literally and figuratively.

On his first jump in the 1988 Calgary Olympics, he fell — and came out in 10th place. But in the years that followed, he kept competing. He barely got a spot on the '92 Olympic team. Then in the Olympic warm-ups he fell. But he went on to win a silver medal.

Wylie said, "I learned to overcome fear by relying on God's acceptance of me . . . You know that God will use you whether you win or lose." When he fails, he tells himself, "OK, this happened to me, but I'm going to learn from this."

Failure needn't be discouraging. Like Paul Wylie, we can use it as a way to learn.

Cast your burden on the Lord. (Psalm 55:22)

Redeemer, help me learn not to go it alone but rather to lean on You.

Measure of health

There are twelve measures of spiritual health that writers and counselors Nancy and Donald Tubesing offer:

- a commitment in LOVE to someone;
- the INTIMACY of sharing and interdependence;
- the vulnerability of TRUST;
- a clear sense of MEANING or DIRECTION in life;
- a HOPE-FILLED vision of the future;
- FAITH-FILLED convictions about the yet-to-be-proven;
- PATIENCE with the ebb and flow of life;
- the sheer delight of heartfelt JOY;
- the use of your IMAGINATION;
- risk-taking, COURAGE; not playing-it-safe; and,
- that appreciation called GRATITUDE.

Work on developing these attitudes in your life. You will be healthier — and not just spiritually. And life will be oh so much richer. Attitudes count.

Strive first for the kingdom of God and His righteousness. (Matthew 6:33)

Keep my eyes focused on You, Your kingdom, Your righteousness, God.

Row, row, row your boat

Joseph Ditler was frustrated with his commute to work in San Diego. He is the development director for the city's Maritime Museum, and his office is on a turn-of-the-century ferry which is docked in the bay. He was tired of fighting the traffic on the way there and especially annoyed because he could see his office right across the bay from his home.

So one day he bought a 15½-foot rowing skiff. Now, at 7:30 each morning, he throws his briefcase and morning coffee into the boat, puts on his Walkman and rows to his job. "It takes about the same time as driving — 30 to 40 minutes — but what a different experience," says Ditler.

If something is frustrating you, perhaps you can approach it from a different perspective. Use your creativity or sense of humor to think things through.

> **Let us also lay aside every weight, and sin . . . and let us run with perseverance the race that is set before us. (Hebrews 12:1-2)**

> *In our frustration, Jesus, give us a share in Your own perseverance.*

Out of adversity, achievement

Dr. Rita Levi-Montalcini shared the Nobel Prize with Stanley Cohen in 1986 for finding the essential factor in nerve cell growth and health.

Born in 1909 into an Italian-Jewish family she had to win her father's permission to study, pass the entrance exam and enroll in the Turin School of Medicine.

Then the rise of Mussolini meant persecution. She conducted her research anyway — in a bedroom lab, in a basement shelter, in hiding.

After the war, Dr. Levi-Montalcini came to the U.S. She eventually collaborated with biochemist Stanley Cohen at Washington University in studies of the nervous system.

"If I had not been discriminated against . . . suffered persecution, I would never have received the Nobel Prize," she says. "You never know what is good, what is bad in life." Adversity can lead to success if we believe in ourselves.

You have seen my affliction . . . taken heed of my adversities, and have not delivered me . . . (to) the enemy. (Psalm 31:7-8)

For the many times You've protected me, thank You, Lord God.

Teach listening — by example

Parents, do you want your children to listen to you? Then LISTEN to them first.

Writer Joan Wester Anderson makes these practical suggestions.

Repeat gurglers', creepers', and toddlers' attempts at speech with genuine delight.

With children under four, explain, explain, explain. Ask and honestly answer questions, too.

From four to six, hear your children out. Look at them directly. Find special times and places for talking. Hear what's behind your children's words.

And from seven on, ask their advice. Put notes under pillows and plates. Use leading phrases to start conversations. Ask for a hug — so you can give them one.

Honest, patient listening. It's the rock on which family life is built.

The patient in spirit is better than the proud in spirit. (Ecclesiastes 7:8)

Unite parents and their teens in mutual, patient listening, Father of our Lord Jesus Christ.

Faith and hope at work

There is more to spreading the Gospel at St. Agnes Parish, Buff Bay, Jamaica, than religious services and education.

In each family, property has been passed through the generations without recording changes in ownership. Rev. Paul Breslin helps the people acquire legal title to their land.

Brother Gerry Hudson runs a chicken co-op to teach chicken farming from egg to chick to bird.

Piglets from the three parish sows are given to local families along with lessons in raising pigs.

And local people raise vegetables on land loaned to the parish for their own use and to sell for profit.

Spreading the Gospel means helping people realize their dignity as children of God. That means giving them the means for a hope-filled future.

Have confidence, because there is hope. (Job 11:18)

Holy Spirit, increase my confidence in the Father's tender loving care for me.

It's really pathetic

When Ronnie Boudreaux paints on the busy sidewalks of New Orleans, he always gets comments. Usually people tell him that his work, which consists mostly of stick figures, is pathetic. But he takes it as a compliment.

The Pathetic movement is the latest trend in the art world. It consists of artwork that looks simple or inept. Some examples include badly rendered drawings or sculpture using rubber chickens or underwear.

Ralph Rugoff, a curator of Pathetic shows, explains the popularity of this art form. He says, "It's supposed to look stupid, or laughable, because it pokes fun at society's fear of failure."

Don't let a fear of failure stop you from following your dreams.

I am the God of Abraham your father; fear not, for I am with you. (Genesis 26:24)

When I become fearful, remind me that You are ever with me to protect and guide me, Lord God.

Youth beats the odds

Luis Parra was born to an unwed teenage mother and never knew his father. As a child he moved around to different places in Mexico and California with his mom and later with his uncle.

Despite his erratic education and home life, Luis has succeeded. The 15-year-old maintains a B-plus average in school, competes on the track and football teams and won a county dance contest. Because of his accomplishments, he recently received the Children's Defense Fund's "Beat the Odds" award.

Luis plans to be a draftsman or an architect. He knows other teens need encouragement to succeed. In a speech he gave for the awards ceremony, he said, "I want them to know they are not alone and there is hope."

Give some encouragement to a teen you know.

Accept whatever befalls you, and in times of humiliation be patient. For gold is tested in the fire, and those found acceptable (to God) in the furnace of humiliation. (Sirach 2:4-5)

How can we encourage teens to bear with present difficulties, God?

The mark of success

Even medications are now being counterfeited. Such fakes are rare, but they're a potential hazard.

Food company president Eric Begleiter has a way to protect consumers from fake drugs. He suggests identifying medicines by holograms — three-dimensional pictures.

Begleiter transferred laser etchings to steel plates. These plates are used to compress powdered sugar into candy mints embossed with holograms.

Powdered drugs could also be pressed into tablets with identifying holograms. These would distinguish real medications from fake.

There are also false ideas of success, which endanger spiritual health. Don't be deceived. The identifying mark of true success is that it contributes in some way to the good of others.

What will it profit them to gain the whole world and forfeit their life? (Mark 8:36)

Teach me, Master, to measure my ideas of success against Yours.

Recycle your reading

We're becoming more and more aware of the need for recycling. Alarming news stories remind us that we're running out of places to dump trash.

But we still throw away lots of things that could be recycled. Books, for instance.

It's wasteful to throw out books in good condition. They can be donated to a neighborhood fund-raising sale, or to a charity thrift shop. Lots of public libraries welcome donated books. So do schools, senior citizens' centers, and prisons.

Elderly or shut-in neighbors might also enjoy reading books that you no longer want.

Make it a practice to give away usable articles instead of discarding them. You'll not only cut down on trash, you'll also help others.

Do not neglect to do good and to share what you have. (Hebrews 13:16)

Inform my generosity with Your grace, Holy Spirit.

From TV to reality: a gap

We know that TV often makes casual sex and violence seem the norm. Does it also distort young people's perception of reality in other ways?

An article in *Omni* magazine comments that fictional TV programs show "easy 22-minute solutions to life crises" and documentaries often show historical events out of context. The article doesn't go into the effect on attitudes, but here are a couple of potential dangers.

An oversimplified picture of human relations can lead young people to expect easy answers to complex problems. Seeing dramatic events without the hard work that went before can lead them to expect instant, effortless success.

Parents can help young people put what they see on TV into perspective.

I will instruct you in the good and right way. (1 Samuel 12:23)

Father, lead parents in Your way so that they in turn can guide the children You have given them.

This, that or the other?

Lots of packaged foods now are designed for people who hate to make decisions, says journalist Molly O'Neill.

Are you torn between meat and cheese? There's sandwich loaf that combines the two.

Not sure which fruit juice you want? Get one of the many fruit-juice blends.

Do you find it hard to decide on a sweet? Just buy ice cream that has chunks of cookies and candy in it.

But it isn't always possible to avoid choosing. There are times when we have to make decisions about matters more important than food. And some decisions are agonizingly difficult. Think it over, talk it over, then do what you have to do. And remember: God is with you.

Who gives heed to the word will prosper, and . . . the wise of heart is called a (person) of discernment. (Proverbs 16:20,21)

Open my ears to Your Word, Lord, so that I may make prudent decisions.

Giving up, getting out

A British burglar had no trouble getting *into* an apartment in Chester. His problem was how to get *out*.

When he started to leave, he found that the door was jammed shut. He couldn't get it open even with an ax.

Finally, he gave up and opened a bottle of Scotch while he waited for the owner to come home and turn him over to the police.

The Scotch this unlucky burglar drank to console himself can also trap people if they become addicted to it. It's easy to get into the habit of alcohol abuse, but hard to get out.

The 12-step method used by Alcoholics Anonymous has shown countless people a way out of addiction.

> **The Lord has anointed me to . . . proclaim liberty to the captives, and the opening of the prison to those who are bound. (Isaiah 61:1)**

Divine Liberator, lead me to freedom.

Jury of teen peers

There is a court in Odessa, Texas, where the lawyers, jury, and defendants aren't old enough to vote or drink. Some are barely legal driving age.

The court is a teen court. Texas law allows teens to judge misdemeanor cases, usually involving drugs or alcohol, traffic violations, or shoplifting. The court seeks to help teens who are shuffled around the regular court system and it also lightens the caseload of the real court. The teen juries give sentences involving community service and jury duty. Upon completion of sentences, charges are dismissed.

The teen court enables the kids to learn more about the criminal justice system and it gives the convicted students a chance at a clean slate after paying for their misjudgment.

Give a teen in your life a second chance — or volunteer some time with a kid who needs one.

A child left to himself brings shame to his mother. (Proverbs 29:15)

What teen that I know, Father, needs my time and loving concern?

A world to care for

Here are some excerpts from a woman's letter to her granddaughter.

"What kind of world will our children and grandchildren — like you — live in?

"The answer . . . lies in the choices we make today . . .

"We should dream of the world through your eyes . . .

"We must learn stewardship . . . Grown-ups, it means living in the world as if it were yours . . .

"We must protect (what keeps) the Earth healthy . . .

"We must work with people around the world to make this globe safe for all life."

What kind of world do you want to live in? Make choices. Dream. Live stewardship. Protect the earth. Cooperate with others for the good of each and all.

The world you live in tomorrow is up to you today.

Refuse the evil and choose the good. (Isaiah 7:15)

Give us a share of Your wisdom, Holy Spirit, so that we may "refuse the evil and choose the good" readily.

Words spoken with hearts and hands

Father Patrick McCahill thinks it's just fine when his congregation doesn't utter a word of response during Mass.

Father McCahill offers a special Mass for the deaf at St. Elizabeth of Hungary Church in Manhattan. He speaks and signs at the same time, but the congregation responds only in sign language. Even choir members "sing" with their hands — in silence.

This special Mass enables the deaf to join fully in the worship service.

There are many other disabilities that make it hard to attend church — from use of a wheelchair to conditions such as Alzheimer's disease. But congregations are finding ways to make churches and services more accessible, to open the doors of the church to all.

Show no partiality as you hold the faith of our Lord Jesus Christ . . . (for) if you show partiality, you commit sin. (James 2:1,9)

Lord whom we worship, enable us to make our churches places of welcome and acceptance for all Your children.

It makes cents

Everybody seems to have spare change lying around in their pockets and purses. Some folks in New York City decided to collect it and put it to good use.

A group of volunteers called Common Cents canvasses apartment buildings, schools, and streets throughout the year, filling sacks with pennies that people don't want. All the money goes to organizations that help the poor, the homeless, and the hungry.

In just 2 years, they've gathered more than $200,000 in pennies and other coins. But that's just a fraction of the $30 million that they estimate is still accumulating in New York City's homes.

Some people are making a big difference with small change.

Do not be hard-hearted or tight-fisted toward your needy neighbor. You should rather open your hand, willingly lending enough to meet the need. (Deuteronomy 15:7-8)

Futher, how may we imitate Your generosity to us?

Putting the church in its place

If you want to reach people with a message, you have to go where they are. That's why Leith Anderson, pastor of the Wooddale Baptist Church in Eden Prairie, Minnesota, decided to go to the mall.

To take advantage of the interest and publicity that the Mall of America was generating with its opening in the summer of 1992, services were held there. 6,000 shoppers and visitors to this country's largest shopping mall stopped to worship together.

"The church is not a building, the church is people," says Pastor Anderson. "When you go out of the building and function as a church, that makes a powerful statement." He sees the modern mall as the descendant of the marketplace where St. Paul preached 2,000 years ago.

In the marketplace, the workplace, or any place else, you can share your faith through the example of your life.

> **I performed many acts of charity . . . I would give my bread to the hungry and my clothing to the naked; and if I saw any one of my people dead . . . I would bury him.**
> **(Tobit 1:16,17)**

> *Lord of the covenant, inspire us to acts of charity and deeds of mercy.*

"Some of God's beauty"

Near Skid Row in downtown Los Angeles is the Catholic Worker soup kitchen. It is nicknamed the "Hippie Kitchen" because of the many young volunteers with long hair.

The kitchen serves three meals a week with food that is donated. The workers live together in a Catholic Worker home. The organization was founded in 1933 and combines Christian ideals with social conscience.

The comments of some of the homeless who eat there make it all worthwhile. "It's nice to see some of God's beauty when you come here," said Laura Williams, a homeless woman. LeeRoy Williamson, also homeless, was very grateful for the food. "If I hit the lottery, I would donate to this place," he said.

Each one of us has the power to bring some of God's joy and love to someone else who really needs it.

Those who believed were of one heart and soul and . . . there was not a needy person among them. (Acts 4:32,34)

Empower me, Holy Spirit, to spread Your joy and love to a needy neighbor.

Make the government your responsibility

Conventional wisdom holds that young people are apathetic about politics and government. But for thousands upon thousands across the land, it's anything but true.

18-year-old Lisa Naegele, who worked for the election of a local candidate, says, "You can't just look at ads and slogans. You have to get involved with it yourself. When you do, you find some of the things people complain about, but you also find a lot of good people trying to make a change."

Susan Straub teaches a popular American Government class at Mother of Mercy High School in Cincinnati. She believes that "young people have to realize that they have a stake in all this. It's their city, their state, their country."

That's true — whatever your age.

Am I my brother's keeper? (Genesis 4:9)

Indeed, God, we are each responsible for the other. May we fulfill this responsibility well and faithfully.

More phrases that praise

Here are some more suggestions for giving your children verbal hugs.

Try phrases such as: "You're Precious!" "Great Discovery!" "Hip, Hip, Hurray!" "Bingo!" "Magnificent!" "Marvelous!" "Terrific!" "You're Important!" "Phenomenal!" "You're Sensational!" "Creative Job!" "You are Responsible!" "You Are Exciting!" "What an Imagination!" "What a Good Listener!" "You are Fun!"

That's only a start.

Here are more ideas: "You're Growing Up!" "You Tried Hard!" "You Care!" "Beautiful Sharing!" "Outstanding Performance!" "You're a Good Friend!" "I Trust You!" "You're Important!" "You Mean a Lot to Me!" "You Make Me Happy!" "You Belong!" "You Brighten My Day!" "I Respect You!" "You're a Joy!" "You're A-OK!" "You Made My Day!"

And once again I ask, "Have you praised your children today?" Remember, the children you praise and encourage today will be tomorrow's self-confident, loving adults.

Praise befits the upright. (Psalm 33:1)

Let my praise be sincere, God.

Gold albums and great goals

Michael W. Smith is one of the hottest names in the music business. The 35-year-old has a gold album and a Grammy for his Christian pop music.

When Smith was 20 years old and starting his music career, he became heavily involved with drugs, alcohol and promiscuous sex. Eventually, he hit bottom and asked God for His help. He straightened his life out and met his wife soon afterward. Today, he is the proud father of five children.

He looks at his past lifestyle and his current career in this way: "Everything good happened to me after getting off the drugs. And God is the most important thing in my life, not my career. If my record bombs, it bombs, but my security is not in my career. *My* goal is to be a great husband and a great father."

And those are great goals to have!

Beloved, if God so loved us, we also ought to love one another. (1 John 4:11)

May love — of You and of family, friends, self — be the goal of my life, Lord of Love.

Another way to win a race

Doctors told Fred Lebow that he had only a few months to live after he was diagnosed with brain cancer. Lebow, who is the director of the New York City Marathon, set out to prove them wrong by running in the 1992 marathon.

Lebow had not run in the Marathon since the early 1970's when it was a race held inside Central Park with fewer than 100 runners. In 1992, the race covered 26 miles of the city and included close to 26,000 runners.

Onlookers cheered and cried as Fred Lebow crossed the finish line with a time of 5:32:34. He beat the odds that many had set against him, and fulfilled one of his dreams.

You can overcome obstacles when you believe that you can. It is when we give up on ourselves that we miss out on the truly great things in life.

Because you have made the Lord your refuge, the Most High your habitation, no evil shall befall you, no scourge come near your tent. (Psalm 91:9-10)

God my protector, help me "beat the odds" against me knowing that You protect and strengthen me.

Hope rises to the top

Bakery workers who'd been laid-off in 1989 bought an unused bakery. Finding the $8 million to finance the purchase was the easy part. Refurbishing a 25-year-old oven took longer than expected. More private financing had to be arranged.

But it was when the ovens began baking 10,000 loaves an hour that problems really began. Bread flew through the air as plastic wrappers popped open a little late. Dough rose too high or baked too long because the assembly line ran late. Six motors burned out. Store orders had to be cut, temporarily. Lifting 100-pound bags of flour for 20 hours, one worker developed a hernia.

But, after this rocky start, 233,000 loaves of bread and packages of buns were baked and quickly bought-up. Things got better. Getting the opportunity to work is sometimes a job in itself.

(The householder said) 'Why do you stand here idle all day?' They said to him, 'Because no one has hired us.' (Matthew 20:6-7)

Master, inspire employers to find room on their payrolls for the unemployed.

The value of a vote

If you have ever thought that it's just too much trouble to vote on election day, let me introduce you to Marian Young of Brooklyn.

Entering the voting booth she made the mistake of moving the lever back and forth. She had in effect voted — without casting her ballot.

The only way for her to get a second chance would be to get a court order. So she set out with a certificate from the voting officials for the State Supreme Court building.

After being sent to several offices, Miss Young finally appeared before a judge. After the court order was granted, the judge addressed the court to say that voting "is worth the effort you have taken today . . . If I were wearing a hat I would take it off to you." Miss Young returned to her polling place to cast her vote in triumph.

How much is your vote worth to you?

We cannot but speak of what we have seen and heard. (Acts 4:20)

Holy Spirit, give me the courage to speak the truth in all circumstances.

Learning respect and harmony

A recent Louis Harris poll found that today's kids believe in racial harmony.

Almost 80 percent of the youngsters said that they want to go to school with someone from another country and 61 percent already do. Over 60 percent said that they would give up some of their pocket money to help kids in poor countries. And for their futures, 85 percent said that they would choose a happy family life over making money.

On the down side, while they credit parents with sharing these values, almost 70 percent of the kids also cited their parents as a major source of prejudice. They learned about stereotypes from the media, other kids at school, and teachers as well.

Children are not born prejudiced — they learn it from others. Be aware of what messages you're sending your kids.

> **There is neither Jew nor Greek . . . slave nor free . . . male nor female; for you are all one in Christ Jesus. (Galatians 3:28)**

> *May mutual respect and toleration be the foundation of our lives, Father - Creator.*

Win-win for volunteers

Computer Media Technology in Mountain View, California, is a big booster of the use of volunteers. About once a week, a staff member takes an afternoon off to do volunteer work — on company time and expense.

The former owner and now consultant to the firm, Clay Teramo, doesn't want employees to "miss out on the intangible rewards. Volunteering helps keep work from becoming a grind."

He sets a good example by donating his own sales and marketing skills for fund-raisers. The company even posts a list of local groups like homes for the elderly or soup kitchens that need help.

Clay Teramo "sees it as a win-win situation."

With some thought and planning, many businesses could encourage employees to volunteer. It's one way of giving back to the communities where we work and live.

Do not hesitate to visit the sick, because for such deeds you will be loved. (Sirach 7:35)

Divine Physician, be with me when I visit the sick, or help anyone who needs my love.

Untangle the grapevine

Whether it's a church council or a business, a community group or a local club, no organization is immune to rumors and suspicion. Bits & Pieces magazine offers these suggestions for dealing with stories that grow too big along the grapevine.

First, try to stay open about everything. Unless secrecy is imperative, give people information. It makes folks feel like part of the team and cuts down on unwarranted speculation.

If a situation looks like it might turn into a problem, deal with it quickly and casually so that a misunderstanding doesn't turn into a rumor.

And remember that you can be suspicious too. Instead of wondering and worrying, go to the source and get the facts. It saves time, worry and ulcers.

What we say and how and why we say it does matter.

Let your speech be consistent. Be quick to hear, and be deliberate in answering . . . Do not be called a slanderer. (Sirach 5:10-11,14)

Holy Spirit, guide my speech so that it will be consistent, courteous and truthful.

Meeting the needs of the sick

Back in 1906 New York's Bellevue Hospital gave milk to needy families.

Today a dozen volunteers and two paid staffers wrestle with five rooms of donated or bought clothes.

Homeless patients need fresh clothing when they are discharged. Those who had their clothes cut away in the emergency room also need clothes on discharge.

Young pediatric clinic patients receive clothes appropriate for the season especially in winter.

Loida Mariscal, who has run the program for 5 years, says, "It's not just a matter of keeping people dressed. We want them to leave with some dignity."

The executive director of Bellevue Hospital, Pamela S. Brier, adds, "Sometimes it takes more to save a life than mere medicine."

Indeed. And sorting, cleaning, repairing and fitting donated clothes is one of them.

If you have many possessions, make your gift from them in proportion; if few, do not be afraid to give according to the little you have. (Tobit 4:8)

Jesus, show me how to be generous and not just with money.

A good deed multiplies

Members of the Indiana Church of the Brethren began Heifer Project International in 1942. In 1992 it celebrated its golden anniversary.

The ecumenical, non-profit, donation supported agency has over all these years supplied meat and dairy cattle, poultry and fish, as well as agricultural training and services to developing areas from Kentucky to Puerto Rico to India.

Rabbits and possibly dairy heifers are going to Poland this year; Romania, next year.

Families helped by Heifer Project are asked to pass on the gift by giving the first-born cow or first dozen eggs to another needy family. A local agency checks compliance.

Faith always seeks to express itself in good deeds. There is a way to help the needy, if we look for it.

Charity is an excellent offering in the presence of the Most High. (Tobit 4:11)

Father, help me imitate to the best of my ability Your own generosity.

Setting and making goals

Sasha Young, a junior at Great Bridge High School in Chesapeake, Virginia, just may have set a precedent at her recent homecoming. The young woman rode in the homecoming parade as part of the queen's court, and then went off to play for her high school football team.

Sasha is the starting kicker for the team and the first female football player for the Great Bridge Wildcats. She tried out for the team just like everyone else and is capable of kicking 30-yard field goals.

She proved herself to the rest of the team through her accuracy and consistency. In turn, they all voted for her to be on the homecoming court.

There may be times in your life when people will tell you that you are not capable of doing something because of your age, your gender, or a physical handicap. Take a risk and prove yourself.

A hoary head is a crown of glory; it is gained in a righteous life. (Proverbs 16:31)

May we respect the aged, the handicapped, and in a special way, women, Creator.

Books beyond price

David Brown, a lawyer fascinated by archeology, was doing field research in Old Harbor, Alaska. One night he went looking for the library. But the last one had been destroyed by fire. Now, there was a library room available, but no money for books.

On his return, he spoke to Pound Ridge, New York, teacher Nancy Freiheit and she to Marilyn Tinter, the library director.

Sales of surplus and donated books are held every two months. Proceeds go to the Old Harbor, Alaska, library.

Other books are shipped book-rate directly to them.

Emily Capjohn, the Old Harbor librarian, says, "We appreciate it so much. They're just wonderful."

Indeed sharing is wonderful. And both giver and receiver grow through the gift given and received.

Those who despise their neighbors are sinners, but happy are those who are kind to the poor. (Proverbs 14:21)

Generous Lord, help us grow through sharing our time, talents and treasure.

Green ways and salad days

Don't think today's teens are airheads just because they wear bizarre clothing or hair styles. Some teens may have green hair, but lots of them also have green thumbs. Millions of teens are interested in gardening and plant care.

In a larger sense, too, young people are our hope for the greening of America. According to a recent survey, the number one concern of today's young people is the environment.

Today, it's children who remind their parents to buy environmentally responsible products, save energy, and so forth.

By the time they reach their teens, many young people are active in environmental projects and groups.

We adults need to follow their lead and take an active part in solving environmental problems.

The Lord . . . formed the earth and made it; He established it; He did not create it a chaos, He formed it to be inhabited! (Isaiah 45:18)

Creator, thank You for the lovely planet which You have given us as our home.

Museum seeks attention

Every year, it seems more and more unusual calendars appear. They offer not just space to record appointments or jot memos, but also photos or drawings of everything from art to wildlife.

The Mutter Museum, part of the College of Physicians in Philadelphia, produced its own "not for the squeamish" 1993 calendar.

Illustrations in it highlight some of the 2,293 objects swallowed by and removed from patients, as well as the X-ray of a toy battleship a child tried to swallow, and the first gallstone operation, June 15, 1867.

Gretchen Worden, curator of the Mutter Museum, says the unique calendar will appeal "to medical historians, med students and fans of fine art photography." It will also make the museum better known.

Being known is never as important as what we are known for.

A good name is to be chosen rather than great riches. (Proverbs 22:1)

What am I known for, Savior?

Surprise gift of love

One '60s November Alice and Bob Blair had 11 little Blairs and a 12th ready to arrive. He did. But then he died and Alice Blair developed pneumonia.

Three days before she was sent home a neighbor who owned a craft shop called Bob Blair. Would he bring all the children to spend a day with her?

"Mom," the children cried the day their mother came home, "do we have a surprise for you!"

There on the shelf above the fireplace was a Nativity scene cast from clay.

Each child told what part he or she had played in its creation. Even 2-year-old Ginger said, "I made the Baby Jesus."

You know, 30 years later Alice Blair says that that Nativity scene "remains one of my most precious gifts."

Love makes a gift memorable, not its cost.

I have loved you with an everlasting love. (Jeremiah 31:3)

Yes, Father, You loved me so much You gave Your Son as my Savior. Thank You.

Behind — literally — today's headlines

Ira Friedman has a master's degree in marketing from Columbia University. He paid his way through school delivering papers. It paid well. He's still at it.

He offers special services. Some of his 3,000 customers are too embarrassed to be seen buying any paper except The New York Times. Mr. Friedman will tuck the customer's tabloid New York Post among The Times' ample folds. It's free for the first four weeks.

The Washington Post, from the nation's capital, can also be delivered with The Times for a fee.

Ira Friedman also supplies his customers with postage stamps at face value. Subway tokens carry a 50 cent delivery charge for a ten-pack.

"Man does not live by The Times alone," he says.

No, women and men live and succeed by being creative at work and at home. What needs your creative touch today?

> **I preferred (wisdom) to scepters and thrones . . . All good things came to me along with her, and . . . uncounted wealth.**
> **(Wisdom of Solomon 7:8,11)**

> *Come, Wisdom of God, fill me with Your treasures.*

In God's image and likeness

These thoughts on family violence come from The Jewish Theological Seminary of America.

"Home should be a haven . . . where you can count on being valued and protected."

"Violence in the family is . . . an abuse of power."

"We are all made in the image of God. (And) to lash out in violence — especially against someone whose life is linked with yours — is to violate a likeness of God, and to degrade that likeness in yourself."

And finally, "look at yourself, at your partner, at your elderly parents, at your children, as images of God. Treat each of them with the respect which that demands."

Home should be where the heart is. If it isn't, get help. Seek protection, or get counseling. But act now.

Your worth comes from God. You are precious in His sight and He loves you.

(God) created all things.
(Wisdom of Solomon 1:14)

For the splendor of my being, God be thanked!

Just too much

There's a stereotype that some adults have of young people: "Teenagers today have too much time on their hands. That's why they get into trouble."

In fact, according to Jim Auer who writes for teens in Liguorian magazine, for too many of our young people just the opposite is true. Like their parents, they are overextending themselves, doing more and more without an end in sight.

Sometimes the pressure comes from well-meaning parents who want their youngsters to take advantage of opportunities to use their talents. Sometimes teens seek a sense of self-worth by staying busy and active. Or, they can't say "no" when asked to participate whether for volunteer work or a party. Then, there are teens who hide problems or fears behind a flurry of activity.

Make time to think about the pace of your own life.

> **Have I not entreated you . . . that you should be My people and I should be your God? . . . I gathered you as a hen gathers her brood under her wings. (2 Esdras 1:28,29,30)**

> *Give me the wisdom to take shelter under Your outstretched wings, Merciful God.*

Keeping your lips sealed

Every person spends a good deal of time listening to others. But sometimes it goes beyond the give-and-take of casual conversation. When we are asked for advice or someone chooses us as a sounding board for a problem, we have special responsibilities.

Certainly members of self-help or prayer groups hear many personal stories. Writer Kay Kinsella points out the seriousness of keeping confidentiality.

"What a great privilege and how awesome it is to be invited to share the secrets of another. Some people tell their secrets to all and sundry — that is their own choice. Even if they do, the fact that we have been consulted seals our lips."

Listening to others unburden themselves of the pains of anger, loneliness, fear, hatred or abuse makes great demands of us. We, in turn, need God's counsel and guidance.

(He) praised the King of heaven, saying . . . from You is wisdom. (1 Esdras 4:58,59)

When others confide in me, share Your wisdom with me, Holy Spirit.

Red and green and . . .

In his book *The Song of the Bird,* Anthony de Mello tells this story:

A minister who was speaking to a class of children asked them: "If all the good people in the world were red and all the bad people were green, what color would you be?"

One little girl thought about it, evidently doing some real soul-searching. Finally, her face brightened and she said, "Reverend, I'd be streaky!"

That little girl understood what we adults sometimes forget: We're mixtures of good and bad, strengths and weaknesses.

When we fall short of perfection, we shouldn't condemn ourselves. God forgives us and loves us, even with our bad streaks.

> **I, I am He who blots out your transgressions for My own sake, and I will not remember your sins. (Isaiah 43:25)**

> *Compassionate Redeemer, help me to forgive others as You forgive me.*

Timely thank you note

Here's a letter written to the editor of a magazine that has a lot to say about gratitude:

"Each year my mother celebrates Thanksgiving in a tangible way by writing a letter thanking someone for something she has been especially grateful for through the years.

"One year she wrote to her high school French teacher, another to the minister who helped us children at college, and another to a man she had never met but who maintained a beautiful rose garden along a street she doesn't often use.

"How much it must mean to these people to know someone appreciates and remembers their efforts."

That note offers much to think about. We needn't wait until Thanksgiving to let people know we appreciate them and what they have meant to us.

(Give) thanks to God the Father at all times and for everything in the name of our Lord Jesus Christ. (Ephesians 5:20)

What can I say, Father, but 'thank You' for all You've graced me with.

Memories — sweet, sad, lasting

The long-running musical, "Cats," features a bittersweet song, "Memories." And memories, bittersweet and glad, are the theme of many a song, article and book.

The holidays are the perfect time to share memories with those you love. Gather together, pull out old photo albums and reminisce.

If grandparents, aunts and uncles are present, they will be an especially rich trove of lore about the fading faces peering out of snapshots and those really antique sepia photos.

As you reminisce, you'll find that the people seem larger than life, characters from a novel. They're part of your memories and the collective memory of those you love.

Share, savor, and celebrate memories, especially at the holidays.

The memory of the righteous is a blessing. (Proverbs 10:7)

Help us treasure our memories — and learn from them, too — Father.

Thanks, good neighbor

Terri Melrose and her husband were involved in a minor Thanksgiving weekend auto accident.

Police officer Wayne Meers brought them to his own home. His wife Nancy welcomed them.

Mrs. Meers allowed them to make necessary phone calls. She drove the Melroses to the local hospital and then to a pharmacy.

After asking if they were hungry — more sore and tired, really — Nancy Meers drove them to their hotel.

She carried their luggage inside. Then she said to call at any hour, no matter how late, if they awakened hungry.

Terri Melrose says, "She gave us much-needed hugs before she left."

There are many ways to be a Good Samaritan. Nancy Meers' was just one way. Be a Good Samaritan, today.

> **The (Samaritan) woman . . . said to the people, "Come, see a man who told me all that I ever did. Can this be the Christ?"**
> **(John 4:28-29)**

> *Jesus, may we imitate the woman of Samaria by announcing to kith and kin that You are the Divine Physician.*

Prescriptions for peace

Most of us want peace. Many of us even work for peace. Think about your own prescription for peace, and consider what these famous people would prescribe:

Mother Teresa of Calcutta says that "if we love each other as God loves each one of us there will be peace."

Actor Robin Williams equates peace with "dignity."

And children's TV host and Presbyterian Minister Fred (Mister) Rogers says that "peace begins with a sense of inner peace . . . from knowing that we are loved by the people who mean the most to us."

What's your prescription for peace? Give your world a dose of it now!

A harvest of righteousness is sown in peace for those who make peace. (James 3:18)

How can I make peace with myself, Author of Peace?

Singing a song with gusto

Lawrence Avery has been cantor for the Beth El Synagogue in New Rochelle, New York, for forty years. Originally he trained to be an opera singer, but when the security of the cantor's job presented itself to the newly-married man, he took it. Then he made it his own.

He is well-known for the interest and zest he continues to bring to his singing and teaching. Cantor Avery has prepared 1,000 Jewish boys and girls for their bar and bat mitzvahs, a ceremony symbolizing their entry into religious adulthood.

The mother of one young student says, "After 40 years, you expect that he knows what he's doing. That's a given. What's remarkable is his enthusiasm. It's not like (my daughter) is his first student, it's like she's his only one."

Enthusiasm for work, for daily living is a priceless gift to those around us as well as to ourselves.

> **Better is a man who works and has an abundance of everything, than one who goes about boasting, but lacks bread.**
> **(Sirach 10:27)**

> *You know the joy and the tedium of work, Carpenter of Nazareth. Help the unemployed to find a job.*

A girl dreams, a horse comes home

Jackie Trentacoste had just begun ninth grade when her family's house burned down. Almost everything was lost.

In the midst of all this Jackie wrote a fantasy about a girl who was given ownership of an Arabian horse she had helped rescue. She entered it in an International Arabian Horse Association essay contest.

Then, one afternoon, a representative from the Association called Jackie to say her fantasy had won first prize.

Jackie and her family flew to Louisville, Kentucky, to meet her prize, Wee Acres Ammal, a 900-pound, white, purebred, 12-year-old Arabian horse.

Dreams can and do come true. As a matter of fact, dreams are the parents of our successes. What are your dreams?

If we hope for what we do not see, we wait for it with patience. (Romans 8:25)

Lord, help me to have a sure hope of accomplishing my dreams.

Not a handicap, a person

A New York City dentist was dismayed when he learned that his newborn son suffered from Down's syndrome and would be mentally retarded.

But he quickly came to love the infant as an individual, just as he did his other children.

He said, "I realized that we *all* have problems and handicaps of one kind or another." No longer feeling hopeless, he began thinking about how modern medicine and education could help his son.

"It won't be easy," he said, "but God gave us our son and will give us the strength and understanding to help him lead a happy life."

Whatever this baby's other handicaps, he will have one great advantage: lots of love and encouragement.

> **I took them up in my arms . . . I led them with cords of compassion, with the bands of love . . . I bent down to them and fed them. (Hosea 11:3,4)**

> *Loving God and Father, how can we extend Your faithful and compassionate love to handicapped infants?*

Striking the right note

Pianist Vladimir Horowitz always had his own piano shipped around with him on concert tours.

On one tour he brought *two* pianos — his own and a new Steinway he used just for a Rachmaninoff concerto.

He pointed out that pianos are delicate instruments and require good care — which they don't always get. Even the weather affects their tone.

Horowitz had an incredibly sensitive ear. He could even detect differences in sound between pianos made in different countries.

Not many of us are so sensitive to sound. But even if we don't have a good ear for music, we can listen carefully in converation. A person's tone can tell us as much as his or her words. Learn to be a good listener.

Let everyone be quick to listen, slow to speak. (James 1:19)

Open my ears, Jesus.

New entertainment, old stories

Some young people are discovering a pre-video form of entertainment. It's called storytelling.

A national Storytelling Festival is now held annually in Tennessee. People of all ages gather to hear stories from a variety of ethnic groups.

Traditional stories provide some good role-models, as well as entertainment. In folktales of all cultures, the hero is usually the little guy who gets out of a tight spot by wit and imagination.

Making up and telling stories is also good therapy for troubled youngsters. It's a creative, nonviolent outlet for their energy.

Storytelling shows young people that creativity doesn't have to involve strobe lights or synthesizers and that problems can be solved by imagination instead of violence.

Tell your children of it, and let your children tell their children, and their children another generation. (Joel 1:3)

Holy Spirit, make us skillful storytellers so that we can pass creativity from generation to generation.

1,200 pound donation

Katie Alward of Granby, Connecticut, is a 4-H Club member who bought Black Velvet, an Angus cross calf. She trained, fed and cared for the steer every day for 18 months. "He was an extra sweet animal," she says.

Then she entered the now 1,200 pound Black Velvet in the West Springfield, Massachusetts, fair. He was named "Reserve Champion" — second among 60 steers.

Afterwards, Katie Alward donated the steer to St. Elizabeth House, a shelter and soup kitchen in Hartford, Connecticut. Paul Laffin, associate director, said, "This really redefines the phrase 'Holy Cow.'"

Slaughtered, Black Velvet's 1,200 pounds yielded 550 pounds of quality meat worth several thousand dollars, for the poor and homeless.

Most of us cannot raise and donate a steer. But all of us can donate something to charity, to people.

It is better to give alms than to treasure up gold. For almsgiving delivers from death. (Tobit 12:8-9)

What can I donate to charity from all You've given me, Lord God?

Consider toys and money and love

December 4

Writer Nancy Barthelemy began really thinking about all the toys her children had while helping them tidy up.

She understood that children need food, shelter, appropriate clothes, support, warmth and love. Using their imaginations, problem-solving abilities and creativity when they play is also crucial.

Thinking about parents, Mrs. Barthelemy found that they need to separate money and all it can buy from love. Parents also need to remember that how they live with their children shows where their hearts are.

And what binds a family together in love? Time. Time spent together.

All this is not to say don't buy any toys for Christmas. Just remember, as Mrs. Barthelemy realized, "all any child really needs is the love and interest of (his or her) parents . . . (nothing) can replace love."

Love is patient and kind; love is not jealous or boastful; it is not arrogant or rude . . . love bears all things, believes all things, hopes all things, endures all things.
(1 Corinthians 13:4-5,7)

Father, enable parents and children to love one another.

"A way of giving back"

If there's a young person in your life, you may be familiar with the musical group, Boyz II Men. They recently set a new record for having a number one song on the charts for the longest time.

These four young men from Philadelphia attract people of all ages and races to their concerts. As 20-year-old member Shawn Stockman says, "We may not be able to change the world, but if we can join people together during a show, it may make a difference in somebody's life."

Boyz II Men also want to have a good influence with their music. Nate Morris, 21, says, "Our values come from our families. We were brought up to believe that God put you in a position to help other people. Music is a way of giving back."

What God-given talents can *you* give back to others?

**There are varieties of service.
(1 Corinthians 12:5)**

Inspire me, Holy Spirit, to put my talents to work in the service of others.

Someone to talk to

Every job has its stresses, but the work of police officers can cause major problems. So to whom does a cop tell his or her troubles?

In Orlando, Florida, a group of volunteer chaplains provide the answer. They listen to officers, radio dispatchers, 911 operators, all the people in the police department who deal with crises and tragedies on a daily basis.

Jack Day, one of the chaplains, believes that "confidentiality is important. It's good to be right with the officer because you get a chance to walk in his shoes. When you walk in someone's shoes, you find out how it feels to be in their position."

So these police pastors take basic training and ride in squad cars to get closer to the officers. Recognizing the feelings and needs of others is the first step to understanding.

You shall not be partial to the poor or defer to the great, but in righteousness shall you judge your neighbor. (Leviticus 19:15)

Open my eyes to see the world through my neighbor's eyes, Holy Spirit.

Our priceless jewel

For thousands of years, jewels have been prized as luxurious gifts.

Recently, one of the gift items in the Neiman Marcus Christmas catalogue was a solid-gold miniature train that carried a load of rubies, diamonds, emeralds, and sapphires. The price was $100,000.

The most valuable and costly gifts are nothing compared to the wonderful gift that we celebrate at Christmas. God gave us a jewel without price — His own Son, who brought us salvation.

As we celebrate God's gift of love, let our gifts to others reflect that love. Let them reflect not our wealth or status, but our concern and love for others.

> **To us a Child is born, to us a Son is given . . . and His name will be called 'Wonderful Counselor, Mighty God, Everlasting Father, Prince of Peace.' (Isaiah 9:6)**

> *Father, You gave me Your Son to be with me in success, joy, sorrow and trial. May I give myself to others in their times of happiness and pain.*

"Healing in Thy wings"

Here is an Advent prayer from the author and minister, Frederick Buechner.

"Thou Son of the Most High, Prince of Peace, be born again into our world.

"Wherever there is war . . . pain . . . loneliness . . . no hope, come, thou long-expected One, with healing in Thy wings.

"Holy Child, whom the shepherds and the kings and the animals adored, be born again.

"Wherever there is boredom . . . fear of failure . . . temptation too strong to resist . . . bitterness of heart, come, Thou Blessed One, with healing in Thy wings . . ."

Each one of us needs the healing touch of Mary's Child. But not all of us think about asking for the gift of healing. And be sure to ask for healing for just one person besides yourself.

The world — and you — will be the better for it.

> **For you who fear My Name the sun of righteousness shall rise, with healing in its wings. (Malachi 4:2)**

> *Son of righteousness, come heal those who most need Your medicine.*

Speaking out for what's right

Navy Lieutenant Paula Coughlin put her career on the line when she decided to speak out on sexual harassment in the Navy.

Lt. Coughlin was one of over 30 women who were abused and assaulted at the Tailhook Association convention in Las Vegas. What angered her most was that these men were her peers and they disregarded the fact that she was a Naval Officer.

She reported the assault to her boss, who did nothing. Lt. Coughlin then took her complaint to the media which set off an investigation of the convention and raised further awareness about sexual harassment in the workforce.

It takes courage to stand up for your rights. Be a person who's helping to make a difference for yourself and others.

> **Do not fear those who kill the body but cannot kill the soul; rather fear him who can destroy both soul and body in hell. (Matthew 10:28)**

Teach us to respect the rights of others, God.

He just keeps swinging

Dennis Walters didn't let a "little thing" like paralysis get in the way of his favorite sport, golf.

Walters lost the use of his legs in a golf cart accident almost 20 years ago. Today he travels 100,000 miles a year conducting golf clinics and showing off his trick shots. He can make shots blindfolded, or from the top of a watch or an egg.

Recently, he became only the fifth person to become an honorary lifetime member of the Professional Golfers' Association of America.

Life sometimes throws us a curve that can put us off track. We can either give in to self-pity or we can follow the example of someone like Dennis Walters.

Try to live your life with creativity and light-heartedness.

> **There is hope for a tree, if it be cut down, that it will sprout again, and that its shoots will not cease. (Job 14:7)**

> *Help me remember that I am rooted in You, Lord my God.*

Four gifts for life

This holiday season some parents will be able to give their children many presents; others, few or none.

But all parents have four presents they can give.

AWE. This is the gift of excited anticipation that looks for the beauty of God and His world.

IDEALS. These are the cure for selfishness and cynicism; they are the measure of a good life.

CONFIDENCE. This means clinging to our vision come what may. Difficulties are part of the worthwhile life.

LOVE. It must mirror God's total, unconditional love for each of His creatures.

To offer your children these four gifts this holiday season is to help make this a better world.

Give the gifts that truly count.

If you then . . . know how to give good gifts to your children, how much more will your Father who is in heaven give good things to those who ask Him! (Matthew 7:11)

Dear Father, help us give each other the gifts that truly count.

Places to try

You're probably familiar with Marlo Thomas. She is the performer who is also the daughter of the late actor Danny Thomas. He was well known for his hard work on behalf of St. Jude's Children's Hospital.

She is also an accomplished stage actress who has done many theatrical productions and has won four Emmys for her TV shows and children's specials. She believes in doing as many things as possible in a lifetime.

When asked how she keeps so active, Thomas replies, "My father used to always say, 'You have to have places to fail.' And what he really meant was: You have to have places to *try* things."

Consider those words in your life, too. Fear of failure can keep you from living your life's dreams.

Never stop trying.

Fear not, little flock, for it is your Father's good pleasure to give you the kingdom. (Luke 12:32)

God, make me brave in the attempt!

Open-hearted giving

For those dependent on the generosity of others, gratitude can become a burden.

Helpers who do things simply and quietly, without making a big deal about what they do, leave the dependent person's pride intact. They don't make the elderly, sick or handicapped individual feel constantly indebted.

One terminally ill man said that "when Christmas came I got more fruit and candy than I could possibly eat. I went door-to-door here in my building and left little packages outside everybody's door. Now that felt good. I was on the giving end for a change."

We all need to be on the giving end at times, just as we all need to allow others to give to us. Graciousness and generosity mean not only doing things for others, but doing them cheerfully. They also mean letting others reciprocate.

Let each of you look not only to your own interests, but to the interests of others. (Philippians 2:4)

Jesus, compassionate Servant-Lord, inspire me to kindness, generosity and gentleness.

Laugh it up

Recent studies have found that children laugh an average of 400 times a day, while adults laugh an average of only 15 times a day.

Some doctors believe that those 385 missing chuckles and giggles could help us lead healthier lives.

Doctors have found that laughter leads to relaxation, reduction of stress, and improves muscle tone and circulation. Twenty seconds of guffawing is the aerobic equivalent of five minutes of hard rowing. Laughter also increases sensory perceptiveness and allows you to perform tasks better.

These studies show that we have to take laughter more seriously.

When we share joyous times with our loved ones, we are doing things that are good for us in more ways than one.

Rejoice with unutterable and exalted joy. (1 Peter 1:8)

Put a smile on my lips, joy in my heart, soul and mind, Holy Spirit.

The work of understanding

It's no accident that people from over 50 different cultural groups live peacefully in New York City's Jackson Heights. They work at it.

Residents there have formed a Cultural Awareness Council to learn about one another's customs — and prevent misunderstandings.

For instance, Black residents once resented what they considered unfriendly treatment in Korean stores. They said Korean cashiers always avoided touching them when they gave back change, and never looked them in the eye. But Koreans explained that in their culture it's rude to touch a stranger or to look people straight in the eye.

Being aware of differences in customs makes for friendlier relationships. Learn more about the different ethnic groups in your community.

Try to not just tolerate, but appreciate your neighbors.

Live peaceably with all. (Romans 12:18)

Holy Spirit, enable us to live in peace with each other and with God.

Constructive criticism and example

Parents can teach their children to be optimistic, says psychologist Martin Seligman.

The most effective way to do it, he points out, is by example. It's important for parents to treat failures and disappointments as temporary setbacks and opportunities to learn. Their positive attitude rubs off on their children. These youngsters are not likely to feel hopeless when they encounter failures in their own lives.

Parents should also be sure their criticism of children is constructive. Telling a child, "You lose everything!" makes him feel hopeless. But saying, "You need to work on keeping track of things," pinpoints a problem that can be solved.

Parents can pass on to their children one of life's most valuable gifts — hope.

Train children in the right way, and when old, they will not stray. (Proverbs 22:6)

Father, inspire parents to guide their children into Your ways.

College students volunteer

Some college students who are troubled by the plight of the poor and homeless are doing something about it.

A program called Into the Streets is one volunteer effort that puts students where their help is needed most. They work directly with adults and children affected by AIDS, homelessness, prejudice, illiteracy, and substance abuse.

The hands-on approach of Into the Streets helps students to better understand other people's situations. As Dan Johnson, a University of Cincinnati junior said, "I worry sometimes about having enough money for school — but there are people out there who don't even have money for the bus."

These charitable young men and women are making a difference for tomorrow's world, today.

Love does no wrong to a neighbor; therefore love is the fulfilling of the law.
(Romans 13:10)

May we respect and help each other, God.

Bad pollution and hot air

Mexican scientists have an unusual plan to deal with Mexico City's air pollution problem. They propose building a hundred giant fans to move the polluted air out over surrounding mountains.

A Texas engineer is among those who don't think the plan is practical. He estimates that the fans could be *built* for about a hundred million dollars, but *running* them would cost several hundred million dollars an hour.

He says that years ago there was a plan to drill holes through the San Gabriel Mountains and blow polluted air out of Los Angeles through them. But calculations showed that running the blowers would take all the power generated in California.

Both cities and individuals need to look at the whole picture before they make important decisions.

> **Which of you, intending to build a tower, does not first ... estimate the cost, to see whether he has enough to complete it? Otherwise, when he has laid a foundation and is not able to finish, all who see it will begin to ridicule him. (Luke 14:28-29)**

Teach us to "look at the whole picture," to count the cost first, Holy Spirit.

Life earns A+

Do you ever wonder just how important your life is to others? How much good you have done?

Syndicated columnist Carl Rowan gave credit to a teacher, Frances Thompson, for providing "a desperately needed belief in myself." His remarks were picked up in a newspaper story and someone sent the article to Miss Thompson.

The teacher wrote to her former student: "You have no idea what that newspaper story meant to me. For years, I endured my brother's arguments that I had wasted my life. That I should have married and had a family. When I read that you gave me credit for helping to launch a marvelous career, I put the clipping in front of my brother. After he'd read it, I said, 'You see, I didn't really waste my life, did I?' "

No one who does good to others wastes a life.

Let your light shine before others, so that they may see your good works and give glory to your Father in heaven. (Matthew 5:16)

May my life sing Your praises, Father.

A gift for the child

Poet Dorothy Herbert has some gift suggestions for Christmas — for others, for the Child in the manger.

"A listening ear to a friend with a heartache / A thank you . . . / Laughter . . . / A kiss and a hug for a handicapped child / Time to read to the sightless / A warm handshake to the new neighbor / An act of kindness to the shut in / A cheery greeting to one who is ill / A smile to the elderly person . . . / A written message to a lonely one . . ."

What presents will you give this Christmas?

What will you give the Child on His birthday?

Give others your self, your time, your love, your compassion, your treasure. And then you will be giving the Child what He most wants — your heart.

> **Opening their treasure chests, (the wise men) offered Him gifts of gold, frankincense, and myrrh. (Matthew 2:11)**

> *Infant God in the manger, I give You my all — I give You my heart.*

Generate your own light

A store in Santa Monica, California, which features environmentally sound products, called for volunteers to help light the store's Christmas tree.

The store, Terra Verde, asked its customers to help out the environment and illuminate the Christmas tree by riding a stationary bike which was hooked up to a generator. Pedaling the bike created power for the lights on the tree. The faster a person pedals, the brighter the lights shine.

Katherine Tiddens, the owner of the store, hoped that it would be an educational experience for kids and adults alike to show them how much energy is wasted each day and how much we take it for granted.

All of us can do our part to protect the environment. Learn more about how you can help. Then let your light shine.

Let mutual love continue. (Hebrews 13:1)

Remind us, Creator, that part of showing mutual love is caring for the environment we all share.

Discouraging all kinds of thieves

So many firs and pines were being stolen for Christmas trees last year that some homeowners came up with a new way to discourage thieves.

They sprayed the conifers in their yards with a harmless colored mixture to make them look unattractive. In a few weeks, the color sloughed off, leaving trees their natural color.

There are also ways to discourage gossips from stealing the good name of others.

When someone repeats malicious gossip to you, just don't reply. Change the subject. If the gossiper persists, say you don't want to talk about the person.

By not listening, you protect the victim of the gossip. You also help the gossiper — who might in time feel shame and guilt for making spiteful comments.

If any think they are religious, and do not bridle their tongues but deceive their hearts, their religion is worthless. (James 1:26)

From gossips and slanderers, and from being gossips and slanderers, God deliver us.

From one generous heart

People give gifts for many reasons: because they feel obligated, or it's a day like Christmas or a birthday that seems to demand it, or simply because of the love of a generous heart.

Here's a story that actor Jack Lemmon tells about Christmas when he was seven. "After my parents and I had opened all of our presents, I ran up the street with a huge box full of my presents to show Frankie, one of my pals. I was not that impressed with what he had received . . . And I also kept looking around for a dog because I knew that was what he had really wanted."

When young Jack Lemmon left, he passed the house of another friend whose father had recently lost his job. The boy was joyfully playing with a puppy — the gift of an unknown friend.

Some gifts cost more than money. They are priceless.

A new commandment I give to you, that . . . even as I have loved you, that you also love one another. (John 13:34)

Let us learn to give the priceless gift of self, generous God.

A light at center of celebration

Lots of us have fond memories of some special way our family celebrated a holiday.

Austrian teenager Edel Cech tells how her family lights its tree on Christmas Eve:

After attending a Christmas pageant in the evening, her family comes home and gathers in the living room. It's dark except for one lighted candle beside the figure of the Christ Child — a symbol that Christ came as a light to the world.

The family says the rosary, and with each prayer, Edel's father lights a candle on the Christmas tree. When the rosary is finished, the whole room is bright, says Edel, like when the angels appeared to the shepherds.

Family customs like this keep the focus on what Christmas celebrates, not just the celebration.

Let us, therefore, celebrate the festival . . . with the unleavened bread of sincerity and truth. (1 Corinthians 5:8)

Holy Spirit, enlighten our celebrations of the feasts and fasts of our faith.

Reflections on Christ's birth

Here are some thoughts on Christ's birth from an ancient prayer book called the Gelasian Sacramentary.

". . . He that was born . . . was a child-God. No wonder . . . the heavens gave tongue, the angels rejoiced, the Magi underwent transformation, kings were seized with anxiety and tiny children were (martyred) . . .

"His mother fed Him (yet) He was the Bread that came from heaven . . . He was laid in the manger like fodder . . . for the animals to eat devoutly.

"There did the ox recognize its owner and the (donkey) its Master's crib; there did (His) people acknowledge Him . . . the Gentiles acclaim Him . . ."

Heady thoughts, But, true.

Do we remember that the Christ Child and His birthday should be the reason for our Christmas parties? For our presents, rich food, fancy desserts and new clothes? And for worship services and kindness to the needy? Merry Christmas!

A young woman shall conceive and bear a son, and shall call his name Immanuel. (Isaiah 7:14)

Jesus, thank You for becoming human so we could be touched by Your divinity.

Inviting others to celebrate

Californians Christine Haenen and Vladimir Huber were married in a simple ceremony and went back to work the next day. A few years later, they decided to finally celebrate with a party. In lieu of gifts, they asked their guests to give at least $20 to one of four different charities.

"What do you do with ten vases?" asked the groom. "This feels better."

As a result, the couple was able to give over $1,500 to good causes. They realized that they had everything they needed while there are many others who have nothing. Their generosity and kindness will give some other people cause to celebrate.

Celebrations can take all forms. We can all try to remember those less fortunate than us at holidays and other special occasions.

**You shall rejoice in your feast.
(Deuteronomy 16:14)**

That we might genuinely enjoy times of rejoicing, Guest at the wedding feast of Cana.

Good goal for a good skate

Casey Pieretti, a 25-year-old high school teacher from San Diego, had his life changed by drunk driving. His father and brother were killed in 1980 by an impaired driver. Five years later, Pieretti was also struck by a drunken driver and had to have his right leg amputated.

In an effort to raise awareness about the dangers of drunk driving, Pieretti has organized a project called "Blade Across America." He and three other people will skate on Rollerblades from San Diego to Washington, D.C. — a 3,500 mile journey.

"If I can skate across the country on an artificial leg, the average person should become more active and set their own physical goals," he said.

That's good advice for any of us. Set a goal for yourself, and meet it.

Wine is a mocker, strong drink a brawler. (Proverbs 20:1)

Give us the wisdom to use alcohol with great moderation, Creator.

Know how to share know-how

Philanthropist Robert Pamplin, Jr., thinks business people have more to give than money. He believes they should also use their expertise to help others.

This Portland businessman and his father give away a substantial amount of their business and personal income. They also devote nearly as much time to philanthropy as to business.

For instance, when the University of Portland was in financial trouble, Pamplin donated nearly half a million dollars. Then he helped raise an equal amount. And perhaps most important, he used his time and know-how to restructure the school's finances to keep the university in the black.

Whether your special talent is managing a business or growing roses, share it with others.

The rich in this world . . . are to do good, to be rich in good deeds, liberal and generous. (1 Timothy 6:17,18)

Help the wealthy, Lord, to use their money wisely with a view to the good of their poorest neighbors.

Keeping Christmas always

Henry van Dyke who wrote "The Other Wiseman" and many other stories for Christmas believed that the holiday spirit could live every day of the year.

Here's what he had to say: "Are you willing to believe that love is the strongest thing in the world — stronger than hate, stronger than evil, stronger than death — and that the blessed life which began in Bethlehem nineteen hundred years ago is the image and brightness of Eternal Love?

"Then you can keep Christmas, and if you keep it for a day, why not always?"

Henry van Dyke was right. Why not keep the light of love and hope that is the heart of Christmas burning from one end of the year to the other?

If you do, you'll have cause to celebrate the joy of each new day, each new opportunity God gives you.

By the tender mercy of our God, the dawn from on high will break upon us . . . to guide our feet into the way of peace. (Luke 1:78,79)

O Infant God in the oxen's stall, my God, my all!

Books in danger from acid and time

All across this country, millions of volumes of literary importance face self-destruction. The enemy is time.

In the past century and a half, there has been a change in materials used to print books. Earlier works were printed on paper made from cotton or linen rags. More recent volumes used cheaper paper made from wood fiber and are high in acid. The result: brittleness and eventual disintegration.

Experts estimate that between 70 and 80 percent of most library collections are in severe danger.

Preservationists are using microfilm, despite its $100 per volume cost to save significant works. Other methods are being studied. And for the future, many publishers are planning to print on acid-free paper.

It's a pointed reminder that what we do today will count tomorrow.

Lay up for yourselves treasures in heaven. (Matthew 6:20)

Master, show me how to live so as to amass lasting treasure — life eternal in heaven.

Generosity from God to us to others

Helen Briggs wrote a thoughtful poem which appeared in "Fellowship in Prayer."

It begins, "God, lead me into quiet ways, / May each daily step bring calm — / A serenity of spirit. / Give of your love to me . . . / guide, and keep me / In need and joy. / . . . Your compassion will surround me / Your strength will add to mine. / Your love will bring me knowledge, peace . . . / the ability to think / And be eternally grateful for the gift of life."

Briggs adds that she asks for these that "I may give to others."

I wonder, do you and I ask God for His gifts to hug them tight? . . . or to be able to share them?

Let's ask God for the gifts we need.

And let's share God's beautifully wrapped presents with others . . . re-wrapped with our unique brand of generosity.

Love may make the world go 'round. But generosity with God's good gifts sustains it.

God loves a cheerful giver.
(2 Corinthians 9:7)

You've enriched me with Your many gifts, God. Enable me to be generous with them.

Also Available

If you have enjoyed this book and are not familiar with other Christopher offerings, here is a brief description.

● **NEWS NOTES.** Over 40 titles are kept in print on a variety of topics and may be obtained in quantity. Single copies of back and future issues are free on request.

● **ECOS CRISTOFOROS.** Spanish translations of popular issues of News Notes. These too can be obtained in quantity. Single copies are free on request.

● **VIDEOCASSETTES.** There are now more than 70 titles in our Videocassette Library. They range from wholesome entertainment to serious discussions on family life, contemporary social issues, spiritual growth and more.

● **APPOINTMENT CALENDAR and MONTHLY PLANNER.** The calendar is large enough to hang on the wall or keep on a desk. It contains an inspirational message for each day of the year and a generous amount of space for daily reminders. The Monthly Planner is handy for pocket or purse, with its practical and attractive design.

Fulfillment brochures and additional information about The Christophers can be obtained by writing: THE CHRISTOPHERS, 12 East 48th St., New York, NY 10017.